Sheila Mickle
"Winter Beach"
11" x 14"   Ink   1985
Prints Available

Sheila Mickle
"Sailing Barnegat Bay"
11" x 14"   Ink   1991
Prints Available

To The Shore Once More

A Portrait of the Jersey Shore

Prose, Poetry, and Works of Art

prose and poetry by
Frank Finale

works of art by

Paula Kolojeski • Dick LaBonté • Theresa Troise Heidel
Ludlow Thorston • Margaret Tourison Berndt • Sara Eyestone
Sheila Mickle • Virginia Perle • Muriel Rogers
Dawn Hotaling • Stephen Harrington

foreword by editor and publisher
George C. Valente

introduction by
Rich Youmans

essays edited by
Louise T. Reynolds

poetry edited by
Thomas Reiter

artwork edited by
George C. Valente
Judy Cardella

graphic design
Judy Cardella

Jersey Shore Publications • Bay Head, New Jersey

Sara Eyestone
"Palace Ponies From Asbury Park"
72" x 48"   Oil   1989
Collection of David and Liz Hagan

For my wife Barbara

and Rich who encouraged me to write these essays

and George whose vision was this book

F. F.

All editorial jointly © 1999 by Jersey Shore Publications,
George C. Valente, and Frank Finale. All artwork © 1999
by featured artists or owners if credited with copyright.

ISBN 0-9632906-1-4
Library of Congress Catalog Number: 98-89077

Printed and bound in Hong Kong
First Edition, July 1999
Second Edition, November 1999

The typeface used for text is Novarese Book
The paper is Shinmorrim A-2 Matt Coated, wt. 157gsm

Jersey Shore Publications
Publishers of:
    Jersey Shore Vacation Magazine
    Jersey Shore Vacation Map
    The Jersey Shore Guide Book
    Jersey Shore Home & Garden
Editor and Publisher: George C. Valente
Post Office Box 176, Bay Head, New Jersey 08742-0176
Telephone: 732-892-1276 • Fax: 732-892-3365
www.jerseyshorevacation.com

Table Of Contents

Contents: Poetry / 4

Contents: Works Of Art / 5

Foreword / 7
by George C. Valente
How This Book Came To Be / 7
About The Artists / 9
About The Essays And Poetry / 9

Introduction / 11
by Rich Youmans

Winter / 15
Winter Still Lifes / 17
Journal From A Snowy Winter: Morning, Noon, And Night / 21
The Kiss / 25
A Fragile Beauty / 29
A Winter's Walk Along The Shore / 33

Spring / 37
The Peepers / 39
The Connection / 43
Class Trip (A Walk Along The Beach) / 47

Summer / 51
Salad Days / 53
To The Shore Once More: Point Pleasant Beach / 57
Summer Job / 61
The Boardwalk: Spring Lake / 65
A Tour Of Spring Lake, Spring Lake Heights, And Sea Girt / 69
To The Sea Once More / 73
Summer Lot / 77

Tales Of Wildlife Along The Jersey Shore / 83
A Telltale Phrase / 83
The Flight Of The Gulls / 84
The Dinner Party / 84
The Geese / 85
A Bit Of Summer Snow / 85
Nature Versus Man / 86

Autumn / 89
Falling Back / 91
The Apple Farm / 95
The Legend Of A Tree: Toms River / 99

Christmas / 103
The Legacy / 105
Assembling The Toys / 109
The Gift Of A Tree / 113
Sally / 117
Old Gray / 121

Poetry / 125
The Jersey Shore / 127
Nature / 136
Autumn / 143
Winter And Christmas / 147
People / 150
School / 156
Labor / 160

Appendix
Stories And Essays / 164
Poems / 164
Other Books And Periodicals / 165

Biographies
Artists / 166
Frank Finale / dust jacket, inside back panel

CONTENTS

Poetry

The Jersey Shore

Twilight Lake / 127
Sea Oats: Island Beach State Park / 127
Seascape: Manasquan, NJ / 127
Reign Of Fire: Asbury Park / 128
River Watch / 128
Point Pleasant Beach / 128
Last Stop / 129
Laird's Applejack (Monmouth, N.J., 1698) / 129
Jersey Shore Vacation Again / 130
The Fishermen: Island Beach State Park / 130
Island Beach State Park / 130
Fishermen / 131
City Girls At Seaside Heights / 131
On The Boardwalk At Point Pleasant Beach / 131
The Galleon / 132
Tail End, Summer / 132
The Return / 132
Separated / 133
Historical Point / 133
In Transit / 133
La Mare / 134

Nature

The Pond / 136
The Violets / 136
The Old Cat / 137
The Claws / 137
Sun Prayer / 137
Storm / 138
Night / 138
My Son Searching For Insects / 138
Spiders / 139
Crow / 139
The Geese / 139
Gulls / 140
Horseshoe Crabs / 140
Unlearning / 141
The House / 141
Sunday / 141

Autumn

The Pumpkin / 143
All Hallow's Eve / 143
The Tormentors / 143
The Age Of Faith / 144
Horror Story / 144

In The Attic / 144
Mass Of Flames / 145
Luck / 145
Necromancers / 145

Winter And Christmas

Windows, Toys & Ice / 147
The Snowman / 147
Walking On Ice / 147
The Firs / 147
From The Corner / 148
Survival / 148
Before Bed / 148
Winter Complaint / 148

People

To My Mother / 150
Louie / 150
Jimmy / 150
The Gathering / 151
Plane Choice / 151
Poe / 152
Making The Rounds / 152
Stranger Passing / 153
Losing God / 153
A Love Poem? / 154
Garage Organist / 154

School

Last Day / 156
Summer Recess / 156
Looking For Miss Gordon / 157
Long Division / 157
Kay Wheeler / 157
Kenny / 158
Elementary / 158

Labor

Julio / 160
Laborer / 160
Construction Worker / 161
The Exterminator / 161
Sign Man / 162
Ritual / 162

C O N T E N T S

Works Of Art

Front Cover: "Spring Lake Boardwalk, Essex And Sussex", Paula Kolojeski

Endpaper #1: "Winter Beach", Sheila Mickle

Endpaper #2: "Sailing Barnegat Bay", Sheila Mickle

2 / "Palace Ponies From Asbury Park", Sara Eyestone

Foreword

6 / "Purr Suit", Margaret Tourison Berndt

Introduction

10 / "St. Catharine's", Paula Kolojeski
10 / "Beach Roses", Paula Kolojeski
12 / "Avon Boardwalk", Paula Kolojeski
13 / "Spring Lake Bridge With Cherry Blossoms", Paula Kolojeski

Winter

14 / "Twin Lights Of Navesink, N.J. 1898", Stephen Harrington
16 / "Christ Church In Shrewsbury", Dawn Hotaling
18 / "Spring Lake At Christmas", Theresa Troise Heidel
19 / "The Ice Cutter", Dick LaBonté
20 / "Barnegat Light, N.J. 1913", Stephen Harrington
23 / "Sandy Hook", Muriel Rogers
24 / "Snow Shower", Muriel Rogers
24 / "Winter Dune", Muriel Rogers
27 / "Early Morning Fishing", Virginia Perle
28 / "The Wreck Of The Susan H. Ritchie, 1894", Dick LaBonté
30 / "An Outing With The Lifesavers", Dick LaBonté
31 / "Lamppost And Benches By The Sea", Theresa Troise Heidel
32 / "Sea Girt Bend, South End", Paula Kolojeski
35 / "Treasures", Ludlow Thorston

Spring

36 / "Another Wonderful Day", Dick LaBonté
38 / "Water Lilies", Sara Eyestone
38 / "Moonstruck", Sara Eyestone
41 / "Julia's Garden", Sara Eyestone
42 / "Ocean View 1895", Dick LaBonté
45 / "Fishing On The Jetty, Jersey Shore", Virginia Perle
45 / "Helping Daddy Fish", Virginia Perle
46 / "New Jersey Coast", Ludlow Thorston
46 / "Atlantic Dunes", Ludlow Thorston
49 / "Summer Of '29", Dick LaBonté

Summer

50 / "Shore Birds", Dick LaBonté
50 / "When Airships Sailed The Skies", Dick LaBonté
52 / "Gull's View", Sheila Mickle
55 / "The Bridal Bridge", Dick LaBonté
56 / "Point Pleasant", Paula Kolojeski
58 / "Spring Lake Surf", Theresa Troise Heidel
59 / "The Inlet", Paula Kolojeski
60 / "Yellow Awnings", Theresa Troise Heidel
63 / "Fourth Of July", Theresa Troise Heidel
64 / "Spring Lake In Early Evening Light", Theresa Troise Heidel
64 / "Flag And Gargoyles, Warren Beach House", Theresa Troise Heidel
64 / "Winter Light, Warren Beach House", Theresa Troise Heidel
64 / "Warren Beach House", Theresa Troise Heidel
67 / "Early Evening Light, Spring Lake Boardwalk", Theresa Troise Heidel
68 / "Blue Reflection", Theresa Troise Heidel

70 / "Spring Lake After A Summer Shower", Theresa Troise Heidel
71 / "St. Catharine's, Spring Lake", Theresa Troise Heidel
72 / "Jenkinson's", Paula Kolojeski
74 / "Under The Boardwalk", Paula Kolojeski
75 / "Bay Head Beach", Paula Kolojeski
76 / "Nineteen Twenty-Three", Dick LaBonté
80 / "Spring Lake Swan Song", Sara Eyestone
81 / "Sea Girt Lighthouse", Paula Kolojeski
82 / "The Glimmer Glass", Paula Kolojeski
87 / "The Marsh In Tuckerton", Paula Kolojeski

Autumn

88 / "The Cove", Paula Kolojeski
90 / "September Beach", Dick LaBonté
92 / "Sea-Esta", Dawn Hotaling
93 / "Sandy Hook Light, N.J. 1886", Stephen Harrington
94 / "Another Season", Ludlow Thorston
96 / "Wicker And Coffee", Theresa Troise Heidel
97 / "Morning Rider", Ludlow Thorston
98 / "Wheels On The Boards", Dawn Hotaling
101 / "Patten Avenue Boats", Dawn Hotaling

Christmas

102 / "St. Catharine's, Christmastime", Theresa Troise Heidel
104 / "St. Catharine's At Christmas", Theresa Troise Heidel
107 / "Victorian Christmas, Spring Lake", Theresa Troise Heidel
108 / "Christmas In Bay Head", Dick LaBonté
111 / "Ocean Grove Christmas", Theresa Troise Heidel
112 / "Change In The Weather", Ludlow Thorston
115 / "Avon Pavilion On A Misty Day", Theresa Troise Heidel
116 / "Asbury Remembered", Theresa Troise Heidel
116 / "Neptune And Seashell", Theresa Troise Heidel
116 / "Carousel Top", Theresa Troise Heidel
116 / "Lantern And Dolphins", Theresa Troise Heidel
118 / "Carrousel", Ludlow Thorston
119 / "Asbury Park Carousel", Paula Kolojeski
120 / "Palace Amusements", Dawn Hotaling
123 / "Ducks In A Row", Margaret Tourison Berndt

Poetry

124 / "Bridge On Shark River, Belmar, N.J.", Theresa Troise Heidel
124 / "Shark River, Early Evening", Theresa Troise Heidel
124 / "Bridge On Shark River, Avon-by-the-Sea, N.J.", Theresa Troise Heidel
126 / "Belmar Gazebo", Theresa Troise Heidel
135 / "Summer Afternoon By The Auditorium", Theresa Troise Heidel
135 / "Ocean Grove Auditorium", Theresa Troise Heidel
135 / "Summer Light By The Tents", Theresa Troise Heidel
142 / "Tents In Early Evening Light", Theresa Troise Heidel
146 / "Quack Attack", Margaret Tourison Berndt
149 / "Sunset On The Toms River", Virginia Perle
155 / "Temperature 62°", Dick LaBonté
155 / "The Bluffs Bar", Dick LaBonté
159 / "Summer Fun", Virginia Perle
163 / "Fisherman's Cove Bait Shack", Paula Kolojeski
163 / "Carlson's Corner", Paula Kolojeski
168 / "Ellen's Dune", Margaret Tourison Berndt

Endpaper #3: "Home From The Sea", Sheila Mickle

Endpaper #4: "Beside The Sea", Sheila Mickle

Back Cover: "Beach Chair", Paula Kolojeski

Margaret Tourison Berndt   "Purr Suit"
48" x 60"   Acrylic   1995   Prints Available

foreword

BY GEORGE C. VALENTE

How This Book Came To Be

In February 1984, at twenty-three, I was less than one year out of college and green as can be at publishing when I created the first edition of COAST *Magazine*. It was digest size, thirty-two pages, and printed in black and a second color of ink, blue. I was enthused and full of energy, and I believed in my concept and vision of a magazine about the history, the people, the arts, and the "feeling" of the Jersey Shore where I had grown up.

I met Frank Finale during the first months of COAST's life. Frank had submitted three poems, *"The Claws," "Storm,"* and *"Separated,"* which were published in the fourth edition (May 1984). Upon reading them for the first time, I became immediately impressed with the quality of the poems; his use of language and imagery brought me to the beach where I could hear a storm, *"the roarer from the sea,"* come ashore; time became audible and visible *"…ticking in the reeds, ticking in the shells, ticking in the claws of the crabs;"* and the irony of man's contemplation of the sad, inevitable unknown was revealed simply: *"above it all, a gull, mocking, mews."* Not only was much of the subject matter a good fit for a magazine about the Jersey Shore, but it also transcended it—the poems held meanings beyond their face-value subject matter. And that was to become evident in much of Frank's work to come, which is now presented in this book. These graceful personal essays and poems capture the essence of the Jersey Shore while exploring universal themes present in life and nature. They elicit a thoughtful contemplation, an emotional response, and a lingering memory.

When I first met Frank, he had a large, dark beard, which gave him the appearance of a lumberjack, or a man who had come of age in the '60s—which he had. I'd speak with him on the phone or he would stop by the office after he submitted more poems. He'd tell me of newly received acceptance letters and rattle off name after name of literary journals and magazines where he would soon be published. He'd tell of places where he was soon to give a reading. And he still tells me of all these things today. When talking with Frank, he always speaks politely and directly about things that matter to him. You feel you are in the presence of a thoughtful and kind man, and, an artist. At last count, he has more than 270 poems and essays published in more than 100 publications.

After six more of Frank's poems were published in COAST during 1984, Rich Youmans, a freelance writer who had written for the magazine, offered to write a profile about him. *"The Poetry And Persona Of Frank Finale"* appeared in the August 1985 edition. In this article, Rich told Frank's life story and revealed his thoughts and influences on his poetry. On "making it" as a poet, Frank said, "You never make it, really. You just keep on writing."

COAST was known as "the magazine celebrating the spirit of the Jersey Shore." Its goal was to capture the quaintness, beauty, mystery, and romance of the Shore. The foundation of COAST's editorial was Jersey Shore history, and in each issue there were historical features and photographs. Also featured were profiles of "old timers" (who would tell of the way things were), resplendent photography, profiles of unique people, features on important current issues, guides to towns as well as fiction and poetry. There were also departments on current events, home and garden, real estate, boating, fishing, art and antiques, day trips, photos from the past, dining out, bed and breakfast inns, and more. Rich Youmans eventually became editor of COAST and, from 1986 through 1991, shaped the finest magazine about the Jersey Shore that has existed to date.

One of the sections in COAST was the "Port O' Call," the last page in the magazine, designed to be a slot for a short personal essay that would evoke memories (and hopefully an emotional response) about some aspect of the Jersey Shore. After two more of Frank's poems, *"Horseshoe Crabs"* and *"The Fishermen: Island Beach State Park,"* were published in November 1985, Rich entailed Frank to write his first "Port O' Call" essay, *"Winter Still Lifes"*—which was published in the November/December 1986 edition, the premier issue of the new, full size, full color COAST. Following that was *"Salad Days"* (April/May 1987), *"To The Shore Once More"* (July 1987), and then twenty-one additional essays and articles as well as numerous poems, all now compiled in this book. Rich worked closely with Frank on the essays and stories, often from initial idea to finished piece, motivating Frank when the ink was not flowing.

I had always thought Frank's essays and poems would make a great book, but when COAST ceased publication in 1992, the idea never came to fruition. Five years later, I was alone on my way to an outdoor art show in Toms River where a friend of mine was displaying. I was interested in seeing other artists' works for possible publication in my new company's guide books, *Jersey Shore Vacation Magazine* and *The Jersey Shore Guide Book*. I hadn't been down that way in a long time, and remembering that Frank had lived in Pine Beach five years ago (as well as my continuing desire to do a book of his work), I thought of giving him a call. By fate, I ran into someone at the show who knew him, and she gave me his phone number. So strong was my desire after years of not communicating, I immediately found a pay phone and called him. From that call, and almost three years of work to come, this book came to be.

In Frank's essays and poems, you will find locations at the Jersey Shore as well as events and situations that may remind you of moments in your own life. From the ebb and flow of the tide to the ebb and flow of relationships, and the human spiritual sense revealed before nature and time, the themes and ideas running through Frank's essays and poems capture the richness of life, all in a Jersey Shore setting.

In the essay, "*The Boardwalk: Spring Lake*," the narrator, unsure of himself and in search of spiritual renewal, describes stepping onto a boardwalk pavilion, the tide moving in and out below.

"I took a deep breath of salt air, let it linger in my lungs, then released it. The wind, laundered by the ocean, felt clean. I stepped onto one of the small, white pavilions which projected about ten yards out onto the beach. The boards underfoot creaked in their nails and below them, the tide rushed in and out, leaving a twisted strand of cargo: shells, driftwood, seaweed, gull feathers, cork, crab bits, and colored glass. Gazing at the foam and bubbles of the sea was dizzying, and I felt as if the whole pavilion was moving forward while the water remained stationary. I sucked in my breath and looked back at the boardwalk for reassurance."

In the story, "*A Fragile Beauty*," the narrator describes how the beauty and inconvenience of an ice storm creates renewed warmth in a couple "*who had not spoken to each other for nearly a week.*"

"As dawn touched the ice-coated windows, they looked upon the world outside. Ice encased each branch, twig, and pine needle. Telephone wires sagged with a cold weight. Bearded with icicles, traffic lights swung lightlessly in blusters of wind. Grasses were as white and lacy as a bride's wedding gown. Everything glistened.

On the radio, the newscaster was warning people not to go out unless it was an emergency. Live wires and tree limbs were down everywhere, and the roads were treacherous. He felt her touch the back of his hand ever so slightly, as they stared out the window in wonder. The room was warm now. The cat was arching its back and nudging their legs."

In "*The Connection*," the narrator, after helping a boy fly his kite, like his father had once helped him, describes the spiritual connection created at certain moments in people's lives:

"I stood there for a few seconds longer, watching the kite, then wished the boy good luck and set off down the beach. Jogging again, I was filled with joy. The sun reflected brilliantly on the ocean, and shells along the tideline winked at me. I kept running, the wind filling my lungs. After a while, I knew if I turned around, the boy would no longer be visible. Yet he remained with me, secured by a string thin and unbreakable."

Rich Youmans explores more of these themes in his introduction that follows.

COAST endured from February 1984 to August 1992, when it ceased publication after three years of failing economy. Although the ending of COAST is one of the hardest periods in my life, I am very proud of the legacy COAST and all of its contributors have left behind. If you page through all seventy-one of its editions (as some libraries and loyal readers still possess), you'll find the histories of most of the towns along the Shore, most major historical events, as well as a record of many unique people who were alive at the time of its publication. It was a mirror to all that the Shore was in the past and all that it was at the time of its publication. Frank's essays and poems are now an integral part of that time and, I believe, of time to come.

I'd like to give thanks to Frank Finale, all of the artists, Judy Cardella, Rich Youmans, Louise Reynolds, and Thomas Reiter.

I'd like to give special thanks to Jane Holand, and especially to my parents, Edith and Frank Valente, for always being there, to whom my work in creating this book over the years is dedicated.

About The Artists

The other equal element within "To The Shore Once More" is the artwork— over one hundred images that, when presented with the prose and poetry, create a complete vision and portrait of the Jersey Shore.

Each of the eleven artists featured in this book is unique in style, approach, and personality. The selection of their images was made with various criteria in mind.

Our goal was not only to show the best work of the artist— which is the case in most of the images presented—but also to take into consideration the combined content of the images as well as the concept that certain images of the Jersey Shore must be included in a book of this type. The six chapter themes also had some bearing on the selections, but no art was chosen to match the content of a particular story. After the selection process, if an image "worked" with an essay, we placed it nearby.

My publishing history with the artists presented is varied; some relationships go back many years to the time COAST Magazine was first published; other relationships were established during recent times with my current company, Jersey Shore Publications, which was founded in 1993. Readers have seen many of the images presented in this book, as well as other images by the artists, in our publications, Jersey Shore Vacation Magazine, Jersey Shore Vacation Map, The Jersey Shore Guide Book, and Jersey Shore Home & Garden.

All of the artists are known throughout the Jersey Shore and some are known regionally and nationally as well. Most of the images, (originals and prints) can be seen in galleries throughout Ocean and Monmouth counties as well as other galleries along the Jersey Shore and throughout New Jersey and the United States. More about each of the artists can be found under the "Biographies" section at the back of this book.

About The Essays And Poetry

All of the articles and essays published here were written for and published in COAST Magazine except for "The Apple Farm" which was originally composed for COAST, but appeared in the Asbury Park Press (September, 25, 1993) and "Sally" which was originally composed for COAST, but first appeared in The Paterson Literary Review (Issue 23, 1993), both about a year after COAST ceased publication.

Of the poems appearing here, many were published in COAST while others have appeared in various anthologies, journals, and magazines. Two of the poems are being presented here for the first time.

During the years COAST Magazine was published (February 1984 through August 1992), the essays were primarily edited by Rich Youmans; a few of these included slight, additional editing by myself.

After COAST Magazine, some of the essays were slightly changed and rewritten by Frank Finale with some additional editing by Rich Youmans.

And finally, in preparation for this book, the essays were edited by Louise Reynolds with some minor, additional editing by myself. Louise Reynolds is the Founding Editor and Editor-in-Chief of the award-winning, independent publication, the new renaissance, an international magazine of ideas and opinions, emphasizing literature and the arts. The thirty-year-old publication is based in Arlington, Massachusetts.

Also, some of the poems were slightly changed and rewritten by Frank and then were edited by Thomas Reiter, a poet and Wayne D. McMurray Professor Of Humanities at Monmouth University in New Jersey. His seventh collection of poems, "Pearly Everlasting" (LSU Press) is scheduled for publication during Spring 2000. He resides in Neptune, New Jersey.

The result is what you are about to read here.

At the end of each essay, you'll see where it was first published. In the "Appendix For The Essays," you'll find full bibliographic information for these publications and books. To see where the poems were first published, refer to the "Appendix For The Poetry."

Paula Kolojeski   "St. Catharine's"
14" x 24"   Pastel   1996   Private Collection   Prints Available

Paula Kolojeski
"Beach Roses"
14" x 18"   Pastel   1991
Private Collection   Prints Available

An Introduction To The Poems And Essays Of Frank Finale

BY RICH YOUMANS

Like one of his favorite poets, Frank Finale sees "the World in a Grain of Sand." His stories and poems abound with telling details, exquisitely told: the *"cuneiform tracks of gulls"* joining his own along a strand; a common egret spied in a salt marsh, *"a bit of summer snow against the tall reeds"*; the *"aroma of sausage, peppers and onions, and God-knows-what sauces"* drifting along a crowded boardwalk ... Frank measures time through these moments and through them lifts and relocates the reader. This is the essence of Frank's gift as a writer and poet: by evoking the often-overlooked details of life, he enables others to see a place—no matter how familiar—as if for the first time.

Rereading these pieces now, I too am transported—not only to various locales of the Jersey Shore, but also to those many nights I spent with Frank at his mahogany dining room table, reading these pieces for the first time. From 1986 to 1991, I served as Frank's primary editor at COAST *Magazine*, where most of these pieces first appeared. I had known Frank prior to this collaboration; we first met in 1984, when I wrote a story about Frank that appeared in COAST in August 1985. I subsequently joined a local poetry group to which he belonged, and a friendship soon developed. The first time I read one of Frank's poems, I immediately recognized his facility with language—which is like saying I immediately recognized a twenty-foot-high neon billboard on a deserted highway. But it wasn't until the "COAST years" that I fully grasped Frank's power as a writer, when he began turning out essays that quickly became reader favorites.

The first essay Frank wrote, *"Winter Still Lifes,"* (November/December 1986) actually stemmed from a request I made for a Christmas poem that could appear in the magazine's "Port O' Call" column. I remember telling him that the piece should be a narrative with good-old fashioned Christmas charm—"maybe something with an elf." Perhaps the addition of the elf proved the ultimate obstacle, but Frank could not produce the Clement Moore piece I envisioned (thank God). He did, however, produce a thoroughly modern essay/prose poem whose few vignettes—from the selection of the family Christmas tree to the ice skating party with *"blurs of bright clothes sliding by"*—leave the reader feeling exhilarated and celebratory.

That first essay spawned many more for COAST—so many, in fact, that several readers thought Frank's last name had to be a pun, since his essays always appeared on the magazine's back page.

(Suffice it to say, Finale is his real name.) I had the privilege of working with Frank on almost all of these pieces, and our editing sessions are still among my favorite memories: Frank and I seated at the dining table, poetry books and literary journals piled at one end; Frank's wife, Barbara (his other editor), grading school papers in the living room; their cat, Shadow, maneuvering around the books and journals with the grace of a second-story man, continually demanding attention. Eventually, Barb would come in and join us, and the night usually ended with all of us gabbing around the table, with Shadow in my lap and another Port O' Call essay in hand.

Some of the pieces Frank wrote are rooted in his youth: the childhood gift of a Lionel train, a white milk car with seven silver cans; his early summer job helping to build houses at the Shore, when he learned to drive a nail into a two-by-four with three swift strokes; the summer after he turned twenty-one, when he drank martinis and busboyed at Martell's in Point Pleasant Beach. Many take their cue from episodes as a husband and father, or as a teacher in the Toms River School System. Others reflect his intense interest in nature. (Two of his favorite books are "A *Pilgrim at Tinker Creek*" by Annie Dillard and *"The Immense Journey"* by Loren Eiseley, classics in the field.)

Yet all of the essays, no matter the topic, derive from Frank's real-life experiences. In most, you see the importance of family in Frank's life: the outings with his children, whether to an apple farm or to an abandoned summer lot; his adventures with Barb, including a memorable kiss on a snowy boardwalk in Seaside Heights; the family Christmas in which distant church bells echo as the Finale children, wildly pedaling in circles, jingle the bells of their new tricycles. Frank has that rare ability to express sentiment without sentimentality, and many of his best pieces are woven from the ties between parents, spouses, and children.

Several essays also reflect Frank's interest in (to quote another of his favorite poets) *"this great wink of eternity."* Frank has a strong mystical side; from the small creatures that hide in bracken salt marshes to the great sweep of ocean under a procession of stars, he finds awe in the immensity of the universe, as well as inspiration. *"I was struck by the preciousness of life in all its varied forms and exalted in being part of that procession,"* he writes in this book's title piece. That pretty much sums up Frank: he exalts in life, and has tried to capture it—in all its varied forms—on paper.

"Nature attracts me," he once told me, "but not the bluebirds-and-flowers type. It's the really amazing and fabulous things, like a cat. If you were from another planet and first saw an animal like the cat, you'd say, 'What an amazing creature!' It purrs, it has claws that can retract—just so many different things. And what is man but a part of nature, anyway?"

The quote is from the story I wrote about Frank back in 1984, and it remains one of my favorites to this day. It shows the unique perspective Frank brings to his writing, which has made his work so evocative, insightful, and memorable. I could say much more, but it's time to let the author speak for himself. Read these stories now, and see if you don't find yourself echoing the closing of that first essay: *"I am glad to be alive...in this land, at this moment."* For my part, I hope Frank Finale brings us many more moments in the years to come.

Paula Kolojeski   "Avon Boardwalk"
18" x 24"   Pastel   1997
Private Collection   Prints Available

Paula Kolojeski   "Spring Lake Bridge With Cherry Blossoms"
18" x 24"   Pastel   1993   Private Collection   Prints Available

TWIN LIGHTS OF NAVESINK,
N.J. 1896 Stephen Harrington
© 1936 STEPHEN HARRINGTON

Stephen Harrington   "Twin Lights Of Navesink, N.J. 1896"
15" x 20"   Composite Ink, Watercolor, and Color Pencil   1996   Prints Available

Winter Still Lifes

I relish those first few chilly days in fall, when squirrels speed up their jittery search for food and clockwork crickets begin to run down and scurry into houses where no one—not even a cat—can find them. The last of the tourists leave the shore, their boats swaying behind them on the dark river of the Parkway. Snow fences design prints of patterned shadows on sand dunes. Amusement arcades no longer amuse—they are boarded shut.

Now come the visits with the children to the apple farms, where gnome-like trees stand in rows and magical fruit is transformed into ciders, pies, and sauces. Watching honeybees fertilize the farm while gathering nectar and pollen, Tim asks, "Where do the bees go in the winter?" Neither his mother nor I could answer. "We'll look it up when we get home. Would you like more pie?"

In Spring Lake, one instant I am looking at a tree, seemingly full this late in fall. The next instant a hundred or more starlings whisk from the bare branches and head south, jerking in unison like bats. They settle and disappear into the horizon of telephone wires, thickening each line. The tree becomes a tree in late autumn again.

Buying the Christmas tree becomes part tradition, part chore, and part joy. The boys and I ride into Belmar to choose our tree from a lot with the largest selection. While waiting for customers, workers huddle near a barrel brimming with flames and pass around a bottle of Christian Brothers brandy. The spicy smell of pine and spruce needles the air.

One of the men appears before us, claps his mittened hands and asks what type of tree we want. Suddenly I flip back to when I was a boy, when workers with red faces and whiskey breath reeled through the smoke-smudged, pine-scented air. My father approaches one and yells, "Let's see your best trees!" He kneels by me and whispers, "Go ahead, pick one; we're going to have the biggest tree on the block!"

Years later, I found myself saying, "Let the boys choose." After twenty minutes of thumping, shaking and spinning trees, the boys pick one I might have chosen years ago.

Later, driving home on snow-muffled Ocean Avenue, we sing, out of tune and much too high, "*Deck The Halls...*"

The next night, on a frozen, freshwater lake, a few blocks from the ocean, children and adults in black or white figure skates glide every which way in the dark. Amazingly, no one collides, though some fall without anyone touching them. Every so often a skate blade catches a streetlamp and winks.

Fires flicker near the shore and people shriek from the sheer exhilaration of traveling headlong through the cold night air.

One of the mothers offers me a cup of hot cocoa. It begins to snow. The whole scene takes on a dream-like quality—blurs of bright clothes sliding by, flakes swirling, steam twisting from my cup—all laced with the giddy sounds of skaters and the whoosh of blades shaving the ice. The snowflakes fall and melt in my cup. I think of the New Year soon to be here and of the old one falling fast away. I am glad to be alive, in the dead of winter, in this land, at this moment.

First appeared in:
COAST Magazine, November/December 1986

Theresa Troise Heidel
"Spring Lake At Christmas"
10" x 14"   1998   Watercolor

Dick LaBonté   "The Ice Cutter"
20" x 24"   1989   Acrylic   Collection of Mrs. D. Carratello   Prints Available

Stephen Harrington   "Barnegat Light, N.J. 1913"
20" x 15"   Composite Ink, Watercolor, and Color Pencil   1996   Prints Available

Journal From A Snowy Winter: Morning, Noon And Night

January 2nd. I am awakened about 3:00 a.m. My wife tells me it's snowing and will continue to snow throughout the morning. At 5:30, school calls: no school. No teaching today.

Later that morning, we dress in our warmest clothes, trudge outdoors and treat our eyes to traceries of snow on dark houses of pines. The Toms River is one long snowfield—the clearest plain I have ever seen. The streets have animal tracks, wide tire tracks, and have metamorphosed from blacktops to whitetops. We crunch and steam our way over to a friend's house. Having moved from Florida two years ago, he was beginning to doubt whether it snowed in this part of New Jersey. Here was crystal proof—and still falling—that buried his doubts.

After coffee and talk, we started home. On the way, two young girls rolling a huge snowball for a snowman shouted hello. Barb asked if they needed help, so the two of us, huffing and puffing, joined them. The snowball grew larger and larger as we rolled it to where they wanted it. It is probably still lying there—a snowball abandoned by a giant—half a snowman waiting for his other half to roll up.

January 14th. It begins to snow about noon today. First, it covered the baseball field, but leaving the playground blacktop black as though it were heated by some secret source. After about an hour, even the playground tops were white—nothing was spared. The frozen tracks and ruts were now smooth, and the sky a whirl of flakes.

When school was finally over, a queue of cars—engines idling, harried mothers waiting—processioned the driveway. Teachers like little steam engines had puffed their way into the parking lot to start their cars and brush the snow off their windows.

A sense of urgency filled the air. On the road, cars with names such as Firebird, Mustang, and Jaguar became docile. One driver goosed the gas in frustration over the slowness of everything. His tires spun, the car swayed, and the snow kept falling.

January 29th. The snow and a harsh winter had killed 2,500 of Washington's troops in Valley Forge; half of Hannibal's men in the Alps; had defeated Napoleon and Hitler in Russia. Had even turned on the Russians when they invaded Finland in the winter of 1939–40.

Snow has its light and life-giving side, too, providing water for streams and rivers, insulation for a hibernating vegetable world, and graceful forms for covering man's environmental mistakes. Snow reveals to us the pleasures of being able to play in, on, or with it. What person could resist the ecstasy of a slide in the snow during his or her lifetime?

February 3rd. Temperature dropped to below zero. Cars would not start. We are deep into the deep freeze of one of the coldest winters ever. No one can stay out long, and hundred-year-old records are broken along with water pipes and overworked heating systems. Our faucets trickle, our fuel bills rise, and the temperature continues to drop.

February 12th. The blizzard is upon us. It began about 2:00 a.m. Monday. Barb went to shut off a light and when returning looked out the window. The street was as dark as the river. The wind off the river shook the pines; she shook her head, "Nothing, yet." Snow was predicted for Thursday and the forecast of snow loomed heavily on Friday and Saturday. Now nothing! Twenty minutes later, the wind and snow woke me. Snow flurried up from the crack in the door on our porch and formed thin drifts. Saharas of white duned the windows and found other cracks—cracks I had not seen before, cracks I had vowed to caulk before winter, and cracks that were forming anew with each blast of wind.

My neighbor's thirty-foot boat sails a sea of snow in his back yard. The birdfeeder tilts with a lump of white; my car, a cave of white, pyramids the driveway. Doilies of ice and snow cover the storm windows, and warnings are up everywhere. Only JCP&L and trucks with plows venture out into this.

I sit before the fireplace, sip hot chocolate, listen to music. Outside a banshee wind wails, and I remember an old curse. Gathering up my robe, I draw closer to the fire.

First appeared in:
COAST *Magazine, January/February/March* 1988

Muriel Rogers   "Sandy Hook"
22" x 30"   Watercolor   1998   Collection of Artist   Prints Available

Muriel Rogers   "Snow Shower"
12" x 30"   Watercolor   1997   Collection of Kenneth Rogers, Jr.   Prints Available

Muriel Rogers
"Winter Dune"
15" x 30"   Watercolor   1997
Collection of Dorothy Kranich

The Kiss

My wife and I, in the throes of the January blahs, had just finished eating supper. We were clearing the table and trying to avoid stepping into each other in our tiny kitchen apartment when she walked over to the steamed-up window. Using a dishrag, she wiped off the condensation and peered out. "Look at it snowing!" she said.

Joining her at the window, I looked out and saw a steady stream of flakes in the street light. When I opened the window, snow whirled in from the darkness. The fresh, cold smell left me giddy. I had looked before and hadn't seen a thing. Now the dark cracks of walkways were filled with white. Ghosts of snow descended on the bones of the three maple trees outside our window and shrubs were little white hillocks.

The town's sanitation department was caught off guard. One lone car, like a bewildered beetle, was feeling its way up the avenue.

We turned toward each other and caught the other's thought. It had been years since we had gone for a walk in the snow just for the sheer joy of it. "Let's do it!" we both seemed to cry at once.

We layered ourselves with clothes—long johns, flannels, sweaters—and topped everything off with hooded coats. Looking and feeling like Arctic explorers minus the dog sled, we abandoned the dirty dishes and set out from the steam-heated, oven-warmed kitchen into the night.

A vast whiteness dwarfed us. Avenues had lost their names. We walked past the Chatfields' yard, where a hapless Chevy pick-up sat on the blocks of its final resting place. The snow had pulled a sheet over its rusted body. We walked past the DeGiorgios', whose once brilliant rose garden was now abloom in white. We trudged down to the muffled roar of the ocean three blocks away.

Running across Ocean Avenue, we plunged into a thigh-high snowdrift and tumbled out, laughing so hard our tears mixed with the snow already melting on our red faces. We crunched our way up to the boardwalk, the cold air burning our lungs as we gasped for breath.

Standing near the shore's edge in the night, there were few points of reference. The only sounds were the soft shushing of the snow and the harsh hissing of the sea. There were no boundaries. Looking up into the swirling night, I grew dizzy and felt as though I might fall off the end of the earth if I didn't grab onto something solid. Gripping the iron railing of the boardwalk, I looked at my wife. Between the flakes I could only see her red hood. Although we were a couple of feet from each other, she barely heard me call out, "Let's go back."

She agreed. What began as a walk in the snow was becoming a survival mission. As we were going, she pulled me into an alcove by a boarded-down hotdog stand. There—unexpectedly—she kissed me.

The white balloons of our breath held no words, but I still remember that simple kiss. Time seemed to stop. Her breath tasted of wintergreen and her lips were moist against mine. The gloom of the alcove lit up. The jasmine scent of her perfume filled my senses and washed away the dank odor of that shelter. Our boots squeaked as we swayed back and forth. Though our faces were numb and the cold and dark engulfed us, this one sweet kiss seemed to prove our existence. Outside the alcove, the snow seethed. Abandoning ourselves to our own weather, we kissed again. I felt at peace with myself and everything around me.

But it was time to leave. The snow, deeper now, fell more heavily and quickly. No cars were out, so we had the joyful experience of galumphing down the middle of the avenue without worrying about traffic. The shells of our ears held an ocean sound, our fingers, feet, and faces tingling like a thousand stars. Wind wolves howled around us and followed us to our door, where we left them. We stayed up into the early morning hours, watched old movies on TV, and made love as the radiator hissed and knocked far into the night.

Originally appeared in:
COAST *Magazine, January/February* 1989
The Beachcomber, August 15, 1998
Anthologized in:
A Loving Voice II: A Caregiver's Book Of More Read-Aloud Stories For The Elderly, 1994

Virginia Perle´   "Early Morning Fishing"
16" x 22"   Watercolor   1995   Collection of Artist   Prints Available

Dick LaBonté   "The Wreck Of The Susan H. Ritchie, 1894"
20" x 30"   Acrylic   1984   Collection of Mr. and Mrs. Herbert H. Wright   Prints Available

A Fragile Beauty

They had not spoken to each other for nearly a week. Perhaps it was the letter to him with a photo of a young model and poet that started the silence. Because she had seen and liked his work, she wanted to meet him, and asked if he would look at her writing. Maybe it was his wife's remark while putting dinner on the table about how incredibly naive he could be. Whatever the reason, the few words that passed between them were sheathed in ice and slippery with double meanings.

It wasn't that they did not love each other. Just last month, he had bought her flowers and had written a silly note for no other reason than she seemed a little depressed over putting on weight. She, that same month, had surprised him one night with his favorite meal, veal scaloppini.

But this month was different. They both arrived home from work more tired than usual. Something would be thrown in the microwave, and they would eat while watching the six o'clock news. Maybe it was the weather: a bone-grinding January with temperatures in the single digits on several consecutive days.

They were tired of the snow that mountained the shopping plazas, tired of the cold and wind-chill, tired of the dark, just tired. They went to bed early and drifted into sleep. He found himself trudging through an unbroken field of white. Where the sky and field met, there was a figure no bigger than a cinder; it seemed familiar to him. He was trying to reach it, but the cold was too distracting. Now he was awake. The dark surrounded him. No streetlights. No night-lights. No sound of the furnace clicking on. No sound except the wind and a steady ticking against the window.

She had already gotten up. He could see her faint outline at the window.

"Why is it so cold?" he asked, wrapping the quilt more tightly around his shoulders.

"Electricity's out," she said.

"What time is it?"

"Five-thirty. Everything is covered with ice."

Getting up, he fumbled for his slippers, his robe, and a flashlight. The cat followed him into the living room and sat by the fireplace.

She came out of the bedroom and took the matches off the mantelpiece. There was a quick, sharp scratch and the room lit up for a split-second. She touched the match to the wicks of the hurricane lamps. The room filled with a wavery glow. He crumpled newspapers and, along with some kindling, put them on the grate of the fireplace. Soon the room held the smell of smoke and the sound of wood crackling and popping.

As dawn touched the ice-coated windows, they looked upon the world outside. Ice encased each branch, twig, and pine needle. Telephone wires sagged with a cold weight. Bearded with icicles, traffic lights swung lightlessly in blusters of wind. Grasses were as white and lacy as a bride's wedding gown. Everything glistened.

On the radio, the newscaster was warning people not to go out unless it was an emergency. Live wires and tree limbs were down everywhere, and the roads were treacherous. He felt her touch the back of his hand ever so slightly, as they stared out the window in wonder. The room was warm now. The cat was arching its back and nudging their legs.

First appeared in:
COAST *Magazine, January/February 1990*

Dick LaBonté
"An Outing With The Lifesavers"
18" x 24"   Acrylic   1982
Collection of Mr. and Mrs. Bruce B. Swenson
Prints Available

Theresa Troise Heidel   "Lamppost And Benches By The Sea"
12" x 16"   Watercolor   1995   Private Collection

Paula Kolojeski   "Sea Girt Bend, South End"
18" x 24"   Pastel   1995   Private Collection   Prints Available

A Winter's Walk Along The Shore

New Jersey's sandy shoreline is geologically older than the rocky coast of New England; here you can almost sense the millions of years of gradual give and take between sea and land. This is especially true of a deserted beach in winter. The crashing of the breakers; the blending of the sky, sea, and sand; and the opulence of space without intrusion leave you feeling like a traveler in time. It might have been a million years ago.

I've always enjoyed walking along a winter's beach, particularly after a northeaster when a roaring surf and wind have stirred up the sea's silty bottom and white breakers have driven ashore a multitude of flotsam not ordinarily seen. It was during one recent walk along the protected sands of Island Beach State Park that I discovered several heavy four-by-fours measuring at least six feet. Studded with white, volcano-shaped barnacles and tangled with brown seaweed, the four-by-fours had been tossed like toothpicks to rest on the sand. I wondered where this timber had come from; once part of a forest, then destined for some man-made structure, they waited now for the slow fires of decay. They were the first of several discoveries on that desolate winter walk.

In the necklace of the tideline lay a variety of shapes, textures, and colors from periwinkles to scallops to jackknife clams; one could spend a lifetime studying them. A few yards down from the timbers, I encountered about a hundred burrfishes, their bodies inflated and almost round, covered with short, stout spines such as a porcupine has. Gazing at them was like looking down from a concert stage at a sea of punk rockers.

And then there were shells—millions of them, stretching as far as the eye could see. Although most were of clams, oysters, and mussels, I also saw moon shells like the shark eye, its half-moon opening partitioned by four whorls. The shark eye, usually colored a

A beach
during the off-season
may be desolate,
but it can also offer
many new discoveries.

You just have to know
what to look for.

glossy brown or gray, derives its name from the central whorl, which is darker than the others, giving it the appearance of an eye.

With the low tide, I could see a multitude of blue mussels exposed along the jetties and pilings. I thought of the "cultivated mussels from certified waters" in hot sauce in my freezer at home. How convenient it is for us now to walk into a supermarket and take them from a deep freezer. I tried to pry a clump of the mussels loose, but the sinewy threads with which they clung to the rocks would not pull free. I stood amazed at the threads' strength and remembered reading somewhere that a scientist was studying the glue that barnacles produce. He thought maybe it could be made synthetically and used to mend broken bones or as a cement in dentistry. I don't know if he succeeded, but I'm sure that someday a use will be found for those tenacious threads.

Walking again along the strand, through the shells' clatter and crunch—a kind of graveyard of the sea—I found a thick piece of rope, the sort used to tie a boat to a dock. I found pieces of cork, and the webbing of a fisherman's net. I found crabs' claws and crab shells. Gull feathers. A mermaid's purse of skate. Bits of sponge.

And, of course, there was beach glass: frosty green, amber, turquoise; from sand they came, and on sand they lie, polished gems twisted with seaweed. Here also were the curves of driftwood carved by the sea and tossed back to land. Odd bits of glass and pieces of wood: What artist could deny this found art? Not a few have spent years trying to get that satisfying combination of shapes and colors. And here they lie on this winter beach, at no cost except the time spent in looking. How long before somebody charged admission? If these objects became valuable enough and profitable enough, I was

certain that someone would devise a way to exploit them. For now, they would remain collectible items for any sharp-eyed beachcomber who wanted to remember the shore's beauty.

Out of the corner of my eye, I caught a shadow moving swiftly in the sand; I turned to look but it had gone. Above me a gull mewed. Birds are one of the constants of the shore, and winter is always a good time to sight the more uncommon species. One of the rarer birds found on Island Beach is the snowy owl. One would not think that this bird, which nests on the Arctic tundra, would wander so far south. But during the years when its main diet of lemmings falls short (about once every four years), this hefty owl with its round, yellow eyes—similar to those of my black cat—finds its way to the Jersey Shore. One need not go out at night to spot them either, since these owls are used to the around-the-clock summer sunlight of the Arctic.

Another rare bird, the black-legged kittiwake, can also be found on Island Beach during the winter. The kittiwake has a solid black triangular tip on its wings, and is the only gull that hovers like a tern, then dives and swims underwater after its prey. It is truly a "sea gull"; it only drinks sea water and it sleeps on the waves, with its head tucked under its wings.

Alone with my reveries, I was startled to suddenly come upon large nests of ospreys, behind the dunes and reeds, on wooden perches that stood almost as tall as telephone poles. The ospreys had nearly been exterminated by pesticides in their food chain, which left the shells of their eggs extremely fragile. Although still on the endangered-species list, they have made a comeback. (The wooden perches, erected by the state, have helped this comeback by offering the ospreys an alternative to nesting on the poles of power lines.) Every year, ospreys add to their nests of sticks, branches, and pieces of sod. Almost six feet across at the base, these are large nests.

Wandering over to one of the high dunes, I saw more osprey nests in the cedar forest that stretched along the island's bayside. All the forest's upper branches, where the osprey nests were lodged, had withered and died off, mainly because sea winds had cracked the branches' bark allowing salt air to lodge in the fissures. Ospreys will weave almost anything—from fishing gear to fish skeletons to seaweed—into their nests, and may even have a family or two of sparrows living in the lower layers of their massive structures.

Returning to the tideline, I searched in vain for frost fish. In my walks on the beach, I've often found starfish and sea horses but only in winter can I find frost fish. The temperature must be in the single digits. The fish, usually whiting stranded during storms, are frozen the instant they wash up on land. A frost fish supposedly tastes better than the usual catch since it was not hooked and did not go through the chemical changes that ordinarily take place. This natural occurrence is similar to our fast freezing peas in order to retain their sweet taste.

I decided to walk back. The only footprints I saw were my own and the tracks of gulls. There were white plumes of breakers on my right and tall, feathery plumes of reed grass on my left. Above me, cirrus clouds streaked the sky. Throughout my winter walk, I am constantly aware of the shore's desolation. At this time of the year, the beach enables you to realize your own capacity for aloneness. Without the constant reminders of civilization, you're nudged into confronting the wintry shore as it is, not as an ad for a vacation or a commercial for suntan lotion. Because no collective *need* has been created for the winter beach, it remains without any *useful* purpose. But it has a rhythm and life of its own that cannot be demeaned by fashionable opinions. The shore in winter is like beach glass, driftwood, and shells: undervalued, passed by, but, in its own stark way, beautiful.

First appeared in:
COAST *Magazine, Winter 1991*
New Jersey Outdoors, Winter 1998

Ludlow Thorston   "Treasures"
5 1/4" x 11 1/4"   Watercolor   1997
Prints Available

Dick LaBonté   "Another Wonderful Day"
40" x 30"   Acrylic   1981   Collection of Mrs. David E. Ritchie   Prints Available

SPRING

April

April comes with the snowdrops and the sound of the peepers. The dead leaves are rinsed by the rain and blown away by the breezes. Squirrels chase each other up and down the trees. Forsythia bushes bloom yellow as the crossing guard's rain slicker. At night, the sound of the ocean seems clearer, its smell more pungent. Though winter may linger for a day or so, one knows it's an April Fool. Easter, Passover, and spring festivals are the mainstays of this month.

Come April, all of life begins to stir. Buds on plants swell and burst. Leaves on trees begin unfurling like a butterfly's wings after emerging from the cocoon. The leaves are light green, tiny and distinct—so new before time and diseases take their toll. Unseen insect eggs break open, and a variety of minute creatures make their way into the world. It is a time for resurrections. On the boardwalk, an old couple sits on a bench sunning themselves. How did I miss the grass turning green again?

May

May is the month of flowers. The grass suddenly is green, and flowers and weeds appear where there was only barren dirt. Hyacinths, dandelions, violets, buttercups, lilies of the valley.... On Mother's Day, it's flowers for Mom. On Memorial Day, there are flags, flowers, and parades of remembrance. Summer homes are repaired, cleaned, and opened. Rental signs spring up everywhere. Arcades along the boardwalk yawn open. It's a month to take joy in being alive.

The vegetable garden has been turned over and limed. Time to plant the tomato seeds again—such an act of faith! The Indians called this month's moon the "Full Flower Moon." Everything seems to be growing and alive, and there are birds everywhere: a robin on the grass running and hopping, jays screeching at the squirrels which frolic from branch to branch, catbirds mewing from the shrubbery, and forked-tail swallows and terns working the river for insects and fish.

Adapted from:
COAST Magazine's 1990 and 1991 Jersey Shore Almanac

Sara Eyestone   "Water Lilies"
30" x 48"   Oil   1995

Sara Eyestone   "Moonstruck"
30" x 54"   Oil   1995
Commissioned by Douglas and Jill Widman

The Peepers

Several years ago, late in March, my wife and I accompanied another couple, good friends of ours, to the cabin they had built in upstate New York. As the car whirred up the New York State Thruway and the radio played "American Pie" endlessly, Darren and Marcy took turns rhapsodizing about their finishing touches to the cabin—screening in the porch, installing central heating, insulating the bedroom. They had spent numerous weekends building the cabin piecemeal—a section of the roof here, a room there—and after several years of planning and working, their vision had become a two-story reality in the Adirondacks. Ironically, as their cabin neared completion, their marriage began disintegrating. This trip was an effort to pull the marriage together: a good weekend with good friends.

And it was. We visited dairy farms and pig farms; met new friends; rode on twisted, foggy mountain roads; passed tumbledown barns with tobacco ads painted on them; played pinball, poker, chess; went hunting for dry wood and new trails; listened to mountain streams, to rain on the roof, and to tales about heroic dogs and unheroic people; drank cold spring water, and watched the sun patch the mountains in a quilt of light and shadow.

Before leaving, we walked around the boundaries of our friends' personal cosmos. The gem in their land, a shimmering pond about fifty feet by twenty-five feet, was fed by an underground spring, and was shallow enough to wade through. Moss and leaves floated on its surface, and at its edge was a rotted tree trunk, half-buried in silt. Pondweeds with spike-like flowers fringed the rim. Pointing to what appeared to be some type of pollution around the weeds, I asked, "What's that?"

"Stay here," Darren said. "I'll be right back to show you."

A few minutes later, he returned from the cabin with a mason jar in hand, excitement in his eyes, and a smile on his face. "That, my city friend, is the beginning of new life. You know those shrill noises you heard when you passed the reservoir last April? These are the creatures that make them."

"These!" The "creatures" were no more than dark, gelatinous dots with an almost tapioca-like consistency.

"Well, not exactly," he said, scooping up a jar full of the dots. "These are their eggs—frogspawn. In another few weeks, they'll develop into tadpoles and then into tiny tree frogs—peepers."

"Then what?"

"They'll do the rest. You'll see—or *hear*, I should say."

Later that day, as we made our way down narrow, serpentine roads and out onto major highways back to New Jersey, I gazed at the lumpish eggs in the mason jar and wondered if they would survive the trip and the new pond in our backyard. Although we had all enjoyed the weekend, I wondered if our friends had resolved the dark side of their marriage. We had heard no arguments.

That spring, I waited for the tadpoles to hatch and for the peepers to peep. I didn't have to wait long. One balmy night when I could not sleep, I went to the back screen door for a breath of air. I heard brief, high-pitched whistles, almost like a jingle of bells, from where a chorus of pipers hid in the reeds of our pond. I woke my wife, and in the dark we listened to the loamy odor of earth's new life as it rose to meet our senses.

A month passed, and the attrition of our daily lives wore away our marvel at the peepers' sound. More concerned with work, money, and schedules, we were discussing which bill to pay and what to do with the left over money when the phone rang. It was Marcy. She sounded choked-up and asked to speak to my wife. I felt I already knew, but I had to ask when my wife put down the receiver forty minutes later.

"What's going on?"

"She's leaving him. Too many broken promises and last night he beat her. She needs a place to stay for a while. Can we...?"

"Sure."

That was years ago. Our friend has remarried and appears happy. Her ex-husband drifted apart from all his old friends, and we have not seen or heard from him since. The pond in our backyard sprung a leak and dried up. We did not fix it, and now it is a pond of leaves.

Yet every spring when night falls, the peepers pipe their bright, brief sounds. Although I have not seen them and am not sure of where they stay (the neighbor's pool?, a nearby river?), they let us know of the resurrection of life. Sometimes under the spell of their music, my mind ripples back to a shining pond in the Adirondacks where love couldn't go wrong. But that was a fantasy brought on by romantic imagination, for all things change, even love. As each generation of peepers inherits the earth, I am left with a reservoir of memories.

First *appeared in:*
COAST *Magazine, May* 1989

Sara Eyestone   "Julia's Garden"
60" x 48"   Oil   1989   Commissioned by the Donald Rotweins

Dick LaBonté   "Ocean View 1895"
24" x 30"   Acrylic   1981   Collection of Mrs. Robert I. Thorburn   Prints Available

The Connection

Out for a morning jog by the ocean, I first spotted the kite about a half mile away. White and diamond-shaped, it bobbed over the beach, dipped, then soared off on a gust of wind that whitecapped the waves. Its bedsheet tail dangled like a string of loose stitches.

As I jogged closer, I saw a boy standing on a dune with a drum-stick of cord in his hand. He was about ten years old, his legs thin as the cross-sticks on the kite he struggled to control. Waving the stick up and down, he looked like a curly-haired maestro, practicing conducting.

I stopped to watch, and as I did my own childhood in Brooklyn came back to me. My father often worked seven days a week; week-days at the local VA hospital, where he usually became frustrated about being unable to admit a needy patient, and weekends when he drove a cab to earn extra money. Yet there existed the rare afternoon when he had free time, and we could spend several hours together. On sunny days, we'd take the green and yellow kite he had given me when I was ten and drive to the park, where we'd battle mischievous breezes and menacing tree branches in the hope of having our kite join the clouds. I would race across the grass, holding the kite above me with outstretched arms, while my father ran beside me with the thin line of string. The kite was almost double my size; I could barely hold it aloft, and sometimes I would trip on the tail. My father would just laugh and tell me to "shake it off" and "get back in the saddle," or some other clichéd advice that was a variation on his basic theme: "It's a dog-eat-dog world, but you can't give up."

And he was right; usually on the third or fourth try, our kite would rise into the deep sky, and the sight of it would make me feel as if I too were flying among the clouds. My father would hand me the string. "Don't let go," he'd say, and I wouldn't.

I had not thought of those fun-filled times for years, those afternoons filled with laughter, frustration, and, ultimately, the joy of seeing our kite ascend. My reverie was interrupted as the wind abruptly diminished and the boy's kite fell with a few long, declining spirals into a nearby dune. It protruded from the compass grass, its thin paper fluttering in the breeze. The boy flung down his drumstick, kicked sand into the air with his bare foot, and plopped himself onto the dune. He rested his chin on his fist like "The Thinker" and stared out at the ocean. His white T-shirt rippled in a sea breeze that had just as suddenly started again.

"Seems like you could use some help," I said, coming up to him.

He looked at me. "Every time I get the kite up, the wind stops."

"The wind looks pretty strong now. Let's try it again. You hold the kite and I'll carry the string. See if that works."

He stood up and brushed the sand off his shorts. "Okay," he said and pulled the kite out of the sand. "Ready?" the boy called, holding the kite as high as he could. About a foot of tail still lay limply on the sand.

We started to run. As I turned to shout, "Let it go!," I stumbled over a large chunk of driftwood and tumbled to the sand.

The boy ran over to me, "Are you okay, mister?" As I got to my feet, I nodded, shaking sand from my shirt and shorts. "I guess I'm not the only one who has trouble," he said, hiding his smile behind his hand.

"Very funny. Let's try it again," I said, this time checking the area in front of me for obstacles. "Ready?"

Again we ran. A gust came off the ocean and caught the kite's frame. The boy let go and the string leaped and became taut. Suddenly I was holding the spirit of the wind. I let out more line and up went the kite, its tail wagging. The higher it went, the more years it pulled from me. I felt ten years old again, flying the kite my father had given me. Then my father appeared, somewhat overweight, sprinting on the sand beside me, beads of sweat glistening on his forehead. "Hold on tight!" he shouted. "Don't let that string go!" My mind soared, high as the gulls. The sea breeze teared my eyes. I kept a firm grip, hearing his voice through the rush of the wind: "We did it! We did it!"

"Hey, mister, we did it!" The boy, not my father, was running beside me, his eyes glistening. I stopped. "Yeah, we did," I said, slightly out of breath. I handed the boy the drumstick and showed him how to work the string, pulling it in a little and letting it back out. The kite now appeared as a speck in the sky. The boy held onto it and smiled.

I stood there for a few seconds longer, watching the kite, then wished the boy good luck and set off down the beach. Jogging again, I was filled with joy. The sun reflected brilliantly on the ocean, and shells along the tideline winked at me. I kept running, the wind filling my lungs. After a while, I knew if I turned around, the boy would no longer be visible. Yet he remained with me, secured by a string thin and unbreakable.

First appeared in:
COAST *Magazine, May 1990*
Raconteur, July 1995
The Beachcomber, July 4, 1998

Virginia Perle   "Fishing On The Jetty, Jersey Shore"
14" x 22"   Watercolor   1997   Private Collection   Prints Available

Virginia Perle   "Helping Daddy Fish"
16" x 12"   Watercolor   1996
Private Collection   Prints Available

Ludlow Thorston   "New Jersey Coast"
5 1/8" x 13 1/4"   Watercolor   1997   Prints Available

Ludlow Thorston   "Atlantic Dunes"
5 1/4" x 11 3/4"   Watercolor   1994   Prints Available

Class Trip (A Walk Along The Beach)

It is early May, and the temperature is in the seventies. Our yellow school bus pulls into the Ortley Beach parking lot, which is empty except for a single car with a Pennsylvania license plate and a shark-like surfboard on its roof. The bus door shutters open and we file out: myself, my class of twenty-seven excited fourth-graders, and school environmentalist Walt Doherty. Leaving our lunches and jackets on the seats, we set off to explore the natural wonders of the Jersey shoreline.

A few early sunbathers look up, surprised, from their novels as we climb onto the wooden boardwalk and descend the few steps to the beach. Our first sensation is an abstract one: Freedom. The visual constriction of highways, buildings, and traffic has vanished. There is a rush of light and a sense of space. The hard angles of buildings and houses have been replaced by smooth curves: dunes, the tideline, waves, the rim of the horizon, the sweep of the gulls. The light on the sea dazzles the eyes, and the waves glitter with a thousand small suns.

By the boardwalk, along the dunes, strands of tall grass have taken root in this loose world of sand. This is our first stop. Gathering around a dune, Walt asks what life we see. A small white butterfly flutters from the grass.

"Insects!" cries one boy.

"Yes. Anything else?"

Raising her hand, one girl shyly says, "Plants."

"Good!" Walt says. "That beach grass spreads out its roots underneath the sand and holds the dune in place."

As I look at the dune where a yellow wildflower peers from the grass, William Blake's lines rise into my thoughts: *"To see a world in a grain of sand,/And a Heaven in a wildflower..."* The sand is multicolored, shiny, and varied in texture and size. Much of it appears to be smoky quartz. I think of how rock is recognized as a symbol of durability, and how quartz is considered one of the hardest minerals. But while rocks wear away and even break, a particle of sand is nearly indestructible. It remains after years of attrition by the weather and the sea. It is the heart of the rock itself—true grit. Perhaps it should become the symbol of durability.

From the grassy dunes, we walk down to the tideline and along the shore between the sea and its high-water mark—a sinuous strand varying from four to eight feet wide, with driftwood, clamshells, molted claws, seaweed, and shells of crabs and mussels as far as the eye can see.

Here we search for other signs of life. We find the cuneiform tracks of gulls on wet, darkened sand and above us, hear their mewing cries. In the strand, we discover gull feathers with their hard, hollow quills and soft barbs—and even a gull's skull picked clean by beetles, its sharp, yellow beak still intact and menacing.

Farther ahead, we spot sandpipers running from the breaking waves. There is a roar, then a cat-like hiss. The sea quickly slides downslope again. The teeter-tail sandpipers turn, searching for small fish and crustaceans as they rapidly chase back the Atlantic. This comic game of tag continues until we get too close. Then, the skittery sandpipers fly off.

We scatter, too, each of us making an individual foray. We regroup at the next jetty to share what we found: a razor clam, a white sand dollar, a skate's black egg purse, scallop and oyster shells, numerous clamshells, and carapaces of crabs. Walt tells us that the coastal Indians made wampum from the white and purple parts of some of these shells. The parts were made into beads and woven into belts or short strands used

for trading. One boy holding an overload of clamshells says, "Wow, I could have been rich!"

Walt laughs, saying, "Yes, but it took a lot of work and craftsmanship to make those shells valuable."

Again we go off on individual excursions. The sun is higher in the sky. The waves are scales of light, and the sky is as clear and distinct as the smell of the salt in the breeze. The children dance back from the waves that rush at their feet. It is a glorious morning.

Just before turning back for lunch, one of the boys finds a horseshoe crab, its underparts exposed to the sun and the gulls. We gather around as it tries to upright itself with its tapered spike. The horseshoe crab has not changed in millions of years, and this one probably would have died if we had not happened along. Walt points out its feeding parts, and mentions that the Atlantic Coast is the only place you can find these creatures. "As frightening as it may look, it is actually quite harmless," he says. Picking it up by its spike, he tosses it back into the Atlantic.

Just past the white foam of the breakers, we see the crab's dark shape moving out to sea. I sense its life force, and realize how intricately and invisibly linked we all are in this ancient world of the shore. The children look on for about half a minute, then turn their attention elsewhere. Above us a laughing gull goes into its noisy "Hah-hah-hah." Walt and I linger for a few seconds, then begin walking with the children back to the bus. The long rhythm of the sea in our ears, the salt air prickling our lungs, we carry with us a renewed awareness of life; somehow our world has grown larger.

First appeared as "A Walk Along The Beach" in:
COAST *Magazine's 1991 Jersey Shore Almanac*
Anthologized in:
Shore Stories, 1998

Dick LaBonté   "Summer Of '29"
20" x 24"   Acrylic   1990   Collection of Bay Head Yacht Club   Prints Available

Dick LaBonté   "Shore Birds"

12" x 20"   Acrylic   1988   Collection of Mr. and Mrs. John Lacey   Prints Available

Dick LaBonté
"When Airships Sailed The Skies"
20" x 24"   Acrylic   1988
Collection of Lori Kupfrian   Prints Available

SUMMER

June

The heavy, sweet fragrance of honeysuckle drifts through the days of June. There are graduations and weddings, barbecues and pool parties. Even Father has his day this month. The longest day of the year is in June, and there seems to be time enough for everything. The green garden hose whooshes with water again. The bees dart about the roses, and strawberries are on their runners. Boogie-boarders dash into the surf and are released from the tedium of the workday week.

The garden needs weeding and the grass cutting. Oblivious to the heat and the honking horns of another wedding, my cat stretches out to match the length of its days. The scent of honeysuckle, roses, and barbecues waft entwined on a warm breeze. On the boardwalks, wheels of chance spin into motion and begin their long summer journey. With the twilight, fireflies spangle the lawn—so many flashing, now here, now there, a silent light show.

July

In July, heat, thunderstorms, and fireworks prevail. The night sky flashes with light and rumbles—a distant thunderstorm or a fireworks display in Seaside Heights? Iridescent-winged dragonflies, some with bodies as blue as the sky itself, skim over lakes and ponds. It is a time for slowing down, for vacations and picnics and watching the gardens grow. The marshes and rivers shimmer with light, and the summer seems as if it will last forever.

In July, teenage boys in raised 4x4 trucks, hard rock music blaring from their stereos, drive by my house and toss firecrackers to show their independence. Their more sedate parents gather at the beach and boardwalk to watch flowers of light open above them, each bloom punctuated by Ohhs! and Ahhs! The sharp odor of powder and damp newspapers hangs in the air. On weekends, the beach is a sea of oiled skins, and the scent of suntan lotion lingers in the tonic of salt air.

August

In lush August, roadsides and meadows are abundant with Queen Anne's Lace, yarrow, chicory, and asters. It is the month of weeds, and of heat so thick that nothing seems to cut through it except the cicadas' high-pitched stutter. The woodchucks are fat and sleek. In the garden, the tomatoes ripen faster than one can eat them. On the beach, brightly colored umbrellas float like lily pads above a lake of sunbathers. Boardwalk stands and arcades crackle with life.

The heat of August shimmers layer upon layer, as the building season reaches its height. Construction workers build a house near the beach; taking off his yellow hard hat, one worker pauses to wipe his brow and watch a child building a sandcastle. On a crowded boardwalk, above the circular lights of the Ferris Wheel, stars sail silently over the ocean. A few blocks away, the lots are loud with frogs and insects pulsating, humming, chirruping. Weeds grow tall by the roadside.

Adapted from:
COAST Magazine's 1990 and 1991 Jersey Shore Almanac

Sheila Mickle   "Gulls' View"
16" x 20"   Acrylic   1995   Collection of George C. Valente   Prints Available

Salad Days

I *believe*

a leaf of grass

is no less

than the journeywork

of the stars

Walt Whitman

When I was six or seven, I felt close to the earth, its plants, and the animals. During the summer months, the garden in our front yard brimmed with life. Tall hedges on three sides set it off from the sidewalks. The house formed the fourth side. With visions of forgotten treasures and tunneling to China, I spent hours digging holes—planting seeds, watching insects, and playing war in that grassy rectangle,

I grew sunflowers taller than myself, with stalks thick as my wrist, their flowers resembling huge, black-eyed susans. Hard to believe that in only three months something so large would spring from something so small.

I remembered how I worked—sweat mingled with dirt blended into brown on my skin—and how the roots of weeds popped when I pulled them. I remember the sound of the spade cutting into moist earth, and the rattle of seeds as I opened the packet.

How long it would be before I planted another seed again. When my mother died of cancer, my father sold the house. He, my younger brother, and I moved into a less green, more urban area, and I grew more concerned with growing up instead of growing plants.

Although I never lost my love for plants and nature, the spirit to plant wasn't rekindled until after I had grown up and had children of my own. The once-verdant courtyard in the apartment complex where my wife and I lived had been left unattended for many years. Once it bloomed with vegetables and roses, lush and beautiful with color. Children from the neighborhood would try to knock down the prized chestnuts from the great horse-chestnut tree that grew there.

But time and too little care had withered the roses, and nobody planted vegetables any more. After spending time in the courtyard with her friends, my wife would have to wash the yard's dust from her face. The foul odor emanating from stagnant water in the two concrete urns that once held flowers exasperated the situation.

Except for the horse-chestnut tree, with its tropical luxuriance and cooling shade, the courtyard had reached its most desiccated point when, a year ago, the complex again changed hands.

The new landlord cared for the yard. He and his wife (Hungarians from South America) tilled the soil, limed it, planted grass seed, tulips, rose bushes, and pansies. They came almost every day before sunset to water the garden and pull up weeds.

With the sound of the garden hose singing to the soil, the spade in the dirt, and the fresh smell of damp earth in the air, a dormant energy swelled in me. Behind our apartment there sprawled a dust-bowl yard, ten yards by ten yards with a projection of another seven by nine feet behind the garage. My three boys—nine, eleven and twelve—tilled the soil, my wife limed it and strung off the area, while I seeded and watered it. We bought a forsythia bush, a lilac bush, and sunflower seeds—Mammoth Russian, the same type I grew as a child. In the small plot behind the garage we planted rows of tomatoes, onions, radishes, and lettuce. Soon my shirt was off, there was dirt under my fingernails, and my dungarees were soiled at the knees.

One morning, after breakfast, I stepped into the backyard and discovered green blades piercing the soil and casting needle-thin shadows. The landlord spotted us and remarked to my wife, "You bring salad, I bring everything else. Have a nice meal in the courtyard for everyone." To pull a salad out of a dust bowl is like pulling a rabbit out of a top hat. I hoped I was enough of a magician to accomplish it.

In May and June the horse-chestnut tree blooms its loveliest, its bread-white flowers speckled with pink and yellow, its large leaves umbrellaing the courtyard oval. We are preparing for our community salad; by the end of July, I hope most of the people who live around the courtyard will come together to share drink, break bread, and celebrate the beauty around them. I hope, too, that my boys will have a memory of the rhythm of life that beats in all growing things.

First appeared in:
COAST Magazine, April/May 1987

Dick LaBonté   "The Bridal Bridge"

20" x 36"   Acrylic   1986   Collection of Mr. and Mrs. David Meehan   Prints Available

Paula Kolojeski   "Point Pleasant"
17" x 24"   Pastel   1996   Private Collection   Prints Available

To The Shore Once More: Point Pleasant Beach

Always, with the salt air, an aroma of sausage, peppers and onions, and God-knows-what sauces drift up and down the boardwalk. It was one of those sea-scintillating summers, every weekend an arcade dealer's dream. I had turned twenty-one, and everything seemed right with the world—I even thought I understood Browning who believed only God could. I drank martinis, busboyed at Martell's, and listened over and over again to Sinatra singing, "It Was A Very Good Year."

Each evening after work, I would put on my best clothes and go back to the boardwalk, looking for the company of girls. Most times I would just pick up the *ping-ping* sounds of pinball machines and the wheels' spinning promises of dolls and teddy bears for a quarter down. The games of skill and chance lured me in, every stand ablaze in neon and crackling its shuttle of numbers.

By day the boardwalk became a different world. In early morning, joggers, bicycle riders, fast walkers, and dog walkers thrived. Some mornings people stayed for about ten minutes to sit on a bench or lean against the rusted railing and stare out at the sea as though waiting for a revelation. Before the beach opened to the vacationing throngs of bathers and sun-tanners, old men went beachcombing; their metal detectors vacuumed the tops of sand ripples like gulls skimming waves. Here and there kids searched for shells, dodged their dogs and the waves or threw stones into the ocean just to test their reach.

Once a dead whale washed up onto the beach. By the time we got there, people had carved their initials into it, put their cigarettes out against its side, and taken chunks of flesh away. One young man climbed on top of the beast and beat his chest like Tarzan. There's something about a dead giant that brings out the worst in people. Because of its smell, the whale was dragged out to sea and blown up, much to the relief of the people who lived nearby.

Other things washed onto shore by the hundreds: blowfish, pink, puffed, and prickly, looking like strange balloons left over from a novelty store; starfish, dry and brittle, which herring gulls liked to strut with in their beaks; and horseshoe crabs, strewn over the tideline and looking from a distance as though some ghostly cavalry had galloped by, leaving only their grotesque shapes.

Storms delivered most of the wreckage. Meanwhile, my own inner storms drove me to the beach—the types of storms that rack many young people on their rites of passage into adulthood: Should I marry the high school girl as my mother urged me to? What would I do when summer ended? What kind of work should I devote my life to? But whatever problems I was weathering dwindled when I brought them before what the poet Hart Crane called "this great wink of eternity." Standing on the shore at night, listening to the hollow boom and hiss of the waves, I stared at the legion of stars processioning the sky. Absorbed by the immensity of space and time, I was struck by the preciousness of life in all its varied forms and exalted in being part of that procession.

First appeared as "To The Shore Once More" in:
COAST Magazine, July 1987
Anthologized in:
Shore Stories, 1998

Theresa Troise Heidel
"Spring Lake Surf"
9" x 14"   1995   Watercolor
Private Collection

Paula Kolojeski   "The Inlet"
17" x 24"   Pastel   1997   Private Collection   Prints Available

Theresa Troise Heidel   "Yellow Awnings"
12" x 16"   Watercolor   1990   Private Collection

Summer Job

When I was a boy and waiting in line with my father to enter the Lincoln Tunnel, he'd turn to me and say, "See this tunnel? I helped build it. Those steel rods..."

"Where, Dad?"

"Well, you can't see them now. They're in the concrete because they're used to reinforce the wall. I used to bend those steel rods. The foreman said I was one of the best steel rod benders he ever had. It took two men to bend one rod, but I used to do it alone."

"How come you still don't do it?"

"Because when the job was done, they laid off most of the men. But you can tell them," he said, rolling down the window to pay the toll, "your father helped build this tunnel." I hadn't dared to ask who he meant by *them*, but I guess it would be my own children; he told the tunnel story with minor variations every time we drove through it.

When roses and honeysuckle perfume the air and my teacher's manuals are shelved away until September, the anxiety of looking for a summer job blossoms in my mind. Years ago, when work was scarce and money scarcer, I took whatever I could get in the summer.

Late one June during the year of a gas crisis, when few jobs were to be had, I picked up work thanks to my older brother. An insurance executive who had connections with builders, he didn't want to hear my mother say one more time, "With your influence and all the people you know, you still can't get your brother a job!" She had a way of bringing this up whenever he had company.

Thus I entered the world of the carpenter's helper, helping to build houses at the Shore. The work was hard, the pay good. When I started I didn't even know how to drive a nail in properly. The carpenter's son took me aside and showed me how to drive an eight-penny nail into a two-by-four with three swift strokes. With practice I was able to swing a hammer well enough to help frame houses. That summer I picked up a new vocabulary (lintel, jamb, stud, joist...), a tan, some muscle, and a raise.

This was a job close to nature even as we were pushing it aside, building houses that pressed farther and farther into the woods, meadows, and wetlands. Somewhere down the road, other developers were doing the same. What would happen when the houses met like railroads connecting east to west, north to south? Where would the deer, foxes, turtles, and possums go?

After lunch on those drowsy summer afternoons, the crew would sprawl on a half-finished porch in the shade of a sassafras tree, make idle conversation about the Mets, watch bumblebees work day lilies, and half-listen to cicadas sizzling in the elms. Eventually one of the crew would pack away the remnants of his lunch, stand up, brush off his pants, and say, "Well, it's that time again." Then a lone hammer would begin to tap, tap, tap, joined by another and another, till the houses resounded with the percussion of hammers. With everyone into the swing of things, I would look back to the porch where we ate lunch. The bumblebees were gone, the cicadas silent.

Helping to build the houses that summer, I also picked up a feeling of satisfaction in a job well done—like my father's feeling of so many years ago. Every once in a while now when I pass the houses I had worked on, I slow down and say to my sons, "See those houses. I helped build them. I left a lot of my sweat and some of my blood there." The boys look at each other puzzled, and my wife says, "We know, you've told us already. Can't you speed it up a little? The people watering their lawns seem more interested in us than in the lawns."

As still another summer and more buildings take the Jersey Shore, I think of those houses long since sold. Houses that have become homes in which children grow up and leave, only to remember their lives spent in those houses. Houses in which adults grow wiser with age and where pets live out their lives. Houses whose exteriors change with passing fashions of color or design. And I feel proud that there is a part of me—my labor, my time, my youth—forever drilled into the framework of those houses. And you can't even see the nails.

First appeared in:
COAST Magazine, June 1988
The Christian Science Monitor, 1991
The Beachcomber, July 18, 1998

Theresa Troise Heidel   "Fourth Of July"
14" x 22"   Watercolor   1995

Theresa Troise Heidel   "Spring Lake In Early Evening Light"
10" x 14"   Watercolor   1995   Private Collection

Theresa Troise Heidel

"Flag And Gargoyles, Warren Beach House"
16" x 11" Watercolor 1995

"Winter Light, Warren Beach House"
10" x 13" Watercolor And Gouache 1996

"Warren Beach House"
13" x 12" Watercolor 1995

The Boardwalk: Spring Lake

I had already been running late for the summer English class I was scheduled to teach when I spilt coffee on my last clean shirt. When I finally left the house, I was rerouted because some of the streets were being repaved. And, naturally, the alternate route was backed up with heavy morning traffic. Aside from my arriving late for class, the morning went smoothly enough but the end-of-day conference with a mother of a girl who was failing, didn't take place. She didn't show up and she hadn't bothered to call. But most disheartening that day was the news that my wife—hospitalized for ten days for blacking out, suddenly and without warning—wouldn't be coming home for another week.

At that point, I knew I needed a respite, a revitalization of my spirits. I drove to Spring Lake which, for me, had always been a serene place, a place where time slowed down a little. Driving up Ocean Avenue along the seaside, I saw the golden cupolas of the new Essex and Sussex hotels shining in the sun. Farther down, a tern passed over the statue of a gargoyle perched grotesquely on top of a three-story Victorian house: evil sea spirits, *beware*.

Adjacent to this was the boardwalk, a two-mile stretch of rickety boards which rose out of the thistle, golden rod, and marram grass anchoring the high dunes. I left my car and walked onto the boards where two song sparrows were chasing each other back and forth. It was still sunny and the wind off the ocean was steady and crisp. A friend of mine once said that the wind here "hollows you out." He was right. I had already begun to feel liberated from the straight lines, boxes, enclosures, and grids of buildings and streets. As I reached the railing and looked beyond the beach to the horizon, I felt a rush of light and an expanse of space. Here sea and sky blend together. I spotted a lone freighter so distant and pale it might have been a phantom.

There are no distracting arcades, amusements, or fast food places on this boardwalk. Here the sounds are elemental: the crash, hiss, and whoosh of water on a smooth beach; the wind playing with the sand and whistling in and out of the spaces of the boardwalk. And always the cries of the gulls which perch themselves on old-fashioned gas lampposts, the kind with quaint lantern tops.

I took a deep breath of salt air, let it linger in my lungs, then released it. The wind, laundered by the ocean, felt clean. I stepped onto one of the small, white pavilions which projected about ten yards out onto the beach. The boards underfoot creaked in their nails and below them, the tide rushed in and out, leaving a twisted strand of cargo: shells, driftwood, seaweed, gull feathers, cork, crab bits, and colored glass. Gazing at the foam and bubbles of the sea was dizzying, and I felt as if the whole pavilion was moving forward while the water remained stationary. I sucked in my breath and looked back at the boardwalk for reassurance.

The slam of a car door broke the mood. A boy and a girl, not more than seven and both squealing, dashed ahead of their parents onto the boardwalk and down the steps to the beach. "Be careful!" their mother shouted, but they were already jumping up and down in the sand, teasing the tide like little sandpipers.

This was one of those summer evenings when people decide to get out of the house and go somewhere. Joggers with Walkmans ran to the music's beat, keeping pace with no one but themselves. Bikers dressed in safety helmets, riding gloves, and day-glo racing shorts avoided knocking into anyone as their wheels thrummed the boards. Children in per-petual motion impatiently pranced a couple of yards ahead of their parents, then, as though playing a game, ran back again.

And then there were couples: man and wife, girl and boyfriend, friend and friend, strolling, talking. The older couples walked with arms linked or hand in hand. Teenagers, with arms around each other's waists, drifted dreamily over the boards' dark cracks.

On one of the barnacled fingers of the jetties, two lovers held hands and watched the herring gulls, their bellies white as breakers, flight smooth as the waves. I watched the lovers while their emotions took wing in a kiss and thought of my wife. Farther out, a fishing boat winked in the sun.

Finding an opening in the boardwalk, I went down to the beach. Each weathered board, according to its age, moaned a different note. In the sky, Crayola-colored fish, dragons, and hawks rippled on the updrafts, each kite invisibly threaded to a child below. Trudging through warm sand and clattering through thousands of bits and pieces of broken mussels, clams, crab shells, and knotted wracks of the necklace left by high tide, I carefully stepped onto the rocks of a jetty. Here I was blessed by the spray from whitecaps and calmed by sea winds. I felt brimmed with space and light.

Turning to leave, a frosted emerald in the strand line caught my eye. I picked it up, brushing off the grains of sand, and held it to the light. It was only a smoothed piece of bottle glass, but for me it had absorbed my mood and this time and place. Later, I would look back on this piece of green glass and smile. As the shadows of the snow fences lengthened along the curves of sand, I pocketed my gift and returned to the boardwalk, thinking, "One week, only one week."

First appeared in:
COAST Magazine, August 1989

Theresa Troise Heidel   "Early Evening Light, Spring Lake Boardwalk"
10" x 14"   Watercolor   1995   Private Collection

Theresa Troise Heidel   "Blue Reflection"
9" x 12"   Watercolor and Gouache   1995   Private Collection

A Tour Of Spring Lake, Spring Lake Heights, And Sea Girt

For me, the soul of the Spring Lake area is the lake itself, with its two wooden bridges arcing over the placid water and reflecting a deeper, wavery version of themselves. Spring Lake, a block in from the thunderous Atlantic on the east and a few blocks from well-traveled Route 71 on the west, is a gem of peacefulness. Willows dip their long, lithe branches into its waters, swans gently wake the surface, and geese rest by the lakeside trees. The lake is emblematic of a certain genteelness that connects the towns of Spring Lake, Sea Girt, and Spring Lake Heights.

History figures prominently in all three towns, from the Victorian architecture of high-peaked gables and widow's walks to the sense of timelessness on each tree-shaded street. The three towns also offer a variety of historic sites. There is the squarish, two-story, redbrick Sea Girt Lighthouse, built in 1896 and currently being restored by the town as an important piece of Jersey Shore history. Two restaurants in Spring Lake Heights, The Old Mill Inn and Eggimanns Tavern, have historic roots: The Old Mill Inn was built on the foundation of a gristmill that dates back to 1720, and Eggimanns, once a highway coach stop, was, according to rumor, a way station for rumrunner's goods during Prohibition.

Spring Lake has two eyecatching structures, one, spiritual, the other, secular. Saint Catharine's double-domed Roman Catholic church towers over Spring Lake's waters. Begun in 1901, the church took six years to complete. To the east of the lake and along the oceanfront is the impressive Essex and Sussex Hotel with its golden cupolas. Dating back to the 1880s, the building takes up a whole block and stands about seven stories tall.

Across from the Spring Lake Train Station and within sight of the lake is another structure which adds to the idyllic quality of this town—a round, white gazebo. The Constitution Gazebo is a relative newcomer to Spring Lake (1987), but it fits in with that slow, serene quality that the town evokes. I can picture myself coming here to sit on one of the benches and read a book, pausing to look up now and then to ponder what I have just read.

The downtown business district has an idyllic atmosphere. People amble from store window to store window, lingering before going on to the next one or perhaps tingling open the door to check out the merchandise. Spring Lake's center runs north, perpendicular to the lake, and is about three blocks long. The scalloped awnings on many of the shops create a colorful beach umbrella effect—warm and sunny even on the grayest days. The business district of Sea Girt, which extends

for two blocks, with no building more than two stories, has a similar small-town quaintness and charm.

Another element the three towns share is a close proximity to the ocean. The boardwalk that runs the length of Sea Girt and Spring Lake, with a break at Wreck Pond between the two towns, is typical of the area: non-commercial, clean, and simple. Walking these boards and staring out into the ocean, I think of how many times the tides have washed this sandy beach, of its many visitors who have listened to this sound before me, and the many who will hear it after I have left. I am struck by the timeless rhythm of it all—the timelessness of the towns behind me, and the eternity of the ocean before me. And when I leave, I feel a sense of renewal, a connection between past and present that the Spring Lake area embodies so well. This is what draws me back, again and again.

First appeared in:
COAST *Magazine, March/April 1990*

Theresa Troise Heidel
"Spring Lake After A Summer Shower"
7" x 8"   Watercolor and Gouache   1995
Private Collection

Theresa Troise Heidel   "St. Catharine's, Spring Lake"
10" x 11"   Watercolor   1992   Private Collection

Paula Kolojeski   "Jenkinson's"
17" x 24"   Pastel   1994   Private Collection   Prints Available

To The Sea Once More

Walking on the Point Pleasant boardwalk from north to south is, as the town's name suggests, pleasant. The boardwalk, which at its northern end offers rows of summer cottages on one side and a wide expanse of beach on the other, widens at Jenkinson's into a panorama of arcades, amusements, shops, and food stands. Here I find places to eat and a variety of smells that perk up my appetite—sweet smells of chocolates and salt-water taffy; spicy smells of sausage, peppers, onions, and pizza; warm smells of bread from hot pretzels; and the sweet, wispy smell of cotton candy. Here arcades crackle with light and the perpetual sound of push-button weapons blasting cosmic targets.

Some afternoons, I come to the boardwalk just to sit on one of the blue and white benches that face the ocean. I read sea poems from a pocket anthology, while the sibilant sea whispers to me to look up and listen to the real thing. When I tire of sitting, I amble over to one of the family arcades and play Skee-Ball or one of the innumerable pinball machines that blink away my quarters in a twinkle of lights.

I walk past the kiddie rides and pause to watch young mothers and fathers waving at children who wave back. The tiny engine which pulls the children clangs its bell and goes around the little park of small, circular rides—a carousel, swings, alligators, ambulances....

I pass by miniature golf courses, frozen custard stands, games of chance. It is not a long walk and already I have left behind the crowds and games. The boardwalk has narrowed. On one side, condos have taken the place of the large houses that once stood here. What few old structures remain are being renovated. On the other side, about fifteen feet from the boardwalk, is a thin strip of dunes, covered with cord grass and encased in snow fencing. Beyond it, beach and ocean seem endless.

Returning to my car, I continue into neighboring Bay Head and am enthralled by the houses along the shore: large, rambling Victorian buildings with steep gables and overhanging eaves, prow-shaped windows and conical roofs. Next to them stand modern homes with daring designs. All have porches and windows facing the ocean.

The beach here is also different. There are more snow fences, dunes, and dune grass to protect the beachfront and homes. The sandy beach seems wilder, freer. There is no boardwalk, only wooden landings at each street entrance which offer the simple pleasure of sitting on a bench and viewing the ocean.

The sound of the ocean is clearer here. There are fewer distracting noises and no hub-bub of people or cars. I can even hear the rustle of grass.

Coming here at night, I sit on the beach. The stars seem like pinholes of light in the sky and the breakers rush in with plumes of white above them. A hollow boom echoes on the sand up and down the shore, then a white hiss of foam bubbles and dissolves. It is the mantra of the sea, elemental, calming. This shore evokes a more primeval world at night, one older than man, and one that will probably outlast him and his creations. It is hard to believe there is a highway only a block away. Rising, I brush the sand off my shorts and head back toward my car, the immensity of it still echoing in my mind.

First appeared in:
The 1990 Guide Book Of The Greater Point Pleasant Area Chamber Of Commerce

Paula Kolojeski   "Under The Boardwalk"
20" x 14"   Pastel   1996
Private Collection   Prints Available

Paula Kolojeski   "Bay Head Beach"
17" x 24"   Pastel   1996   Private Collection   Prints Available

Dick LaBonté   "Nineteen Twenty-Three"
20" x 24"   Acrylic   1983   Collection of Mr. and Mrs. Edwin C. Andrews, Jr.   Prints Available

Summer Lot

Empty lots are never really empty. They are filled with chance vegetation: blue chicory, Queen Anne's lace, thistle, pods of milkweed. And you can always find some man-made debris—styrofoam cups, yellowed supermarket advertisements, flat beer cans, an endless stream of American litter. In these lots, our childhood imaginations loomed large. We played hide-and-seek, tag, soldiers, explorers.... On the edge of civilization as we knew it, these wildflower lots lured us from the grids of cement walks and asphalt streets, into a world of greenery which buzzed, hummed, and whirred with hidden lives.

I had forgotten about such lots until late one summer Saturday several years ago, when my wife, Barbara, asked me to drive her and the boys to the supermarket. Once there, she took six-year-old Steven into the store while the other two—Mike, ten, and Alan, eight—stayed with me in the car. I found shopping a tedious affair and was happy to be relieved of it. I had brought along the first volume of *Remembrance Of Things Past*, and the boys had a few toys with them—Alan, his Matchbox cars, and Mike, a squadron of small plastic soldiers.

Absently I gazed at the empty, cyclone-fenced lot across the street, then settled into my reading. After about half an hour of *Remembrance*, I looked in the rearview mirror and caught Mike's soldiers making an unprovoked attack on Alan's convoy of trucks and cars. Alan protested by running a jeep into Mike's hand. Outside, shopping carts shimmered in the parking lot as the sun reached its zenith. As the air in the car grew heavy with heat, I decided it was time to do something else.

"Let's stretch our legs and go to the lot across the way," I said. Opening the car door, the boys hopped out. "What about mom?" Mike asked.

"We'll be back before she is. We'll do some exploring. You never know what you'll find in an empty lot."

The lot measured about a square block. Although it was fenced off from the parking spaces, a section of the six-foot barrier had a hole where the wire mesh was curled aside like the top around a key on a sardine can. Between scrub pines, tall weeds, and shrubbery, a narrow dirt path snaked its way into the interior. The perimeter of the lot was strewn with broken crates, drifts of old newspapers, jagged bottles, cans that had long since quenched someone's thirst, and a rusted cart that lay upside down, its four wheels in the air like a dead animal.

As we entered, a blue jay screeched and flew to a pine farther in along the trail. We began exploring. Mike was the first to find something when a glint of sun along the side of the path caught his eye. At first he thought it was just a bottle cap. Reaching over to pick it up, he realized it was a dime. Encouraged by his find, Mike knelt down and closely scanned the path.

"Maybe someone had a hole in his pocket," he said as he pried another coin out of the path and inspected it. "Hey, an Indian head penny! This could be worth money—they don't make these anymore!"

Alan was about five yards down the path making his own discoveries. He picked up a large square of cardboard soggy from the last rain. "WHOA!!" he screamed as he threw it down and pedaled back three quick steps, nearly losing his balance.

"What's the matter?" I yelled, running over to him.

"Zillions of roaches!" he cried, grimacing and backing away even farther from the cardboard lying in the path.

With the two boys standing behind me, I cautiously lifted up one corner of the limp cardboard. Like tiny mechanical toys, crickets sprang and crawled for cover under rocks and weeds. Within half a minute, they had all disappeared into the landscape.

"Those aren't roaches, they're crickets," I said, half smiling.

"Whatever they are, they're too many for me," said Alan.

"What a jerk," Mike mumbled.

"If you really want to see insects, just lift up any stone and look," I said.

Finding one stone about the size of a loaf of bread, I turned it over to reveal its damp underside. Out rolled a hairy, red centipede. When I was a child, my family lived for about a year in a dank basement apartment where spiders and centipedes proliferated. For me they took on a sinister aspect, to the point where I would not go to bed unless my father swore he had cleared my room of these alien creatures. Once, as an adult, my wife's false eyelash in the middle of our bed sent me into a panic. Now, suddenly seeing a centipede crawl over my hand, I shrieked and dropped the stone onto the path. Sow bugs rolled themselves into balls like little armadillos and played dead. Ants scurried into holes. Mike stepped over, picked the centipede off my hand, and placed it on a nearby leaf.

"It's okay now, Dad," he said.

I nodded, struggling to regain my composure. "That's enough about insects for today," I mumbled and started up the path once again.

We explored a while longer. I pointed out the molted, dry husk of a cicada on the bark of a pine. The boys remarked how much the husk looked like a giant fly. As if on cue, we heard a cicada's shrill stutter high in the trees.

"Hey Dad, I think Mom might be back by now," Mike said.

"Yeah, you're probably right," I said. "Let's follow the path out."

At the end of the trail, we found ourselves at the other end of the parking lot. Alan was still about ten yards behind us picking a flower off a shrub.

"Hurry up, slowpoke!" Mike yelled.

Alan caught up, and we left the lot together. As we stepped through the torn fence, I spotted a flash of blue in a nearby pine, then heard a screech as the jay flew back into the lot. We headed back toward our car.

I was satisfied I had shared with the boys some of my fascination for empty lots and the things one might find in them. Barb and Steven returned to the car shortly after we did, and we all pitched in loading the trunk with groceries. After settling into the car, Barb asked how we entertained ourselves while she was shopping. I said we went exploring.

Mike mentioned the money he found and told about my episode with the centipede. Then Alan proudly held up his discovery. In his hand was a brown egg sac attached to a twig. The sac had a rough, papery texture and looked like dried foam. His little brother Steven tried to grab it.

"Hey, hands off, this is mine!" Alan yelled, jerking his hand away.

"Just be sure you put it in a jar and put a lid on it. And keep it in your room," his mother said, looking at it skeptically. "What kind of insect made such a sac?" she asked, but no one knew.

When we got home, we put the groceries away. Mike cleaned off and filed his Indian head penny into his coin collection. Alan found a mayonnaise jar under the sink and brought the jar and egg case to his room.

As summer ended, the boys spent most of their time finishing schoolwork, playing with their friends, and watching TV. The days grew colder, the nights longer. Christmas came and went. During the middle of an exceptionally balmy March, Alan asked one morning if I remembered that empty lot I had taken them to.

"Of course I do. Why?"

"Well, I forgot the lid."

"What lid?"

"To the jar."

"What jar?"

"The one that mom told me to put the egg sac in."

Leading me to his bedroom, with his mother and two brothers following, Alan pointed toward his dresser. The wall behind it pulsated with tiny, green praying mantises instinctively seeking out their places in the world. The source of all this wiggling life was the foam-like egg sac in the mayonnaise jar on Alan's dresser. The cracked sac was alive with miniature mantises bubbling out and spilling onto the dresser top. Down the sides and up the wall they went.

In the doorway behind me, Mike pleaded, "You can't kill them, Dad. My teacher said there's a fine if you kill them."

"Quick!" I shouted. "Get some jars—but with lids!"

Out came the jars from cupboards above the stove, from shelves under the kitchen sink, from ledges in the pantry— mason jars, jelly jars, and spaghetti-sauce jars. In went the mantises. We scooped them with glossy magazines and our hands; a number of the mantises slipped through the cracks in the floorboards and between the walls, but we caught most of the others. Mike, who had just finished studying insects in school, told his brother not to worry because praying mantises eat other insects, and people use them in their gardens to help get rid of pesty bugs. After reading up on his newest pets, Alan set up a natural habitat of leaves and grass in each jar. Each day he fed the mantises bits of raw hamburger to curb their carnivorous appetites and moistened them with water.

That spring whenever we visited friends who had gardens, Alan would bring a jar of mantises as a present.

"They're good for the garden. They eat pests," he would tell the somewhat taken-back host and hostess.

Most often, the couple would allow him to turn the mantises loose in the backyard while they supervised from the patio. Alan would return with a smile on his face and an empty jar in his hand. "Well, that's another one," he would whisper to his mother and me.

Since then, many springs have slipped glittering into summers, and many summers have burned away to fall. Alan, now the age I was then, has a wife and a child of his own. Although he left his insect days behind, the mantis egg case—now brittle to the touch—remains in a jar on the shelf in his den, a dusty testimony to life's unexpected turns.

First appeared in:
Without Halos, Volume VIII, 1991
COAST Magazine, Summer 1991

Sara Eyestone
"Spring Lake Swan Song"
36" x 72"   Oil   1997
Collection of Dr. and Mrs. A. Cohn

Paula Kolojeski   "Sea Girt Lighthouse"
17" x 19"   Pastel   1991   Private Collection   Prints Available

Paula Kolojeski   "The Glimmer Glass"
18" x 24"   Pastel   1993   Private Collection   Prints Available

Tales Of Wildlife Along The Jersey Shore

A Telltale Phrase

When I first moved to Pine Beach in southern New Jersey, I was surprised to see few sidewalks, many vacant lots, but an abundance of natural beauty. I grew up in Brooklyn, where my vision was blocked by buildings and the greenery buried by asphalt. The little nature left was divided among postage-stamp backyards, token parks, and sidewalks where huge trees seemed to grow out of the concrete.

By contrast, the shore had miles of sandy beaches and unobstructed views. Inland, although rapidly changing because of development, there was ample greenery—woods, meadows, marshes. The sense of space lifted my spirit.

Back in Brooklyn, the wildlife I was familiar with consisted of birds (mostly sparrows and pigeons), bedraggled stray cats, dingy dogs, squirrels, and mice. At Pine Beach, I saw creatures I had never seen before: muskrats, otters, chipmunks, and raccoons. So I was more startled than surprised when my wife who had gone to get a box from the cellar landing, suddenly screamed, "Come quick! There's a dead animal!"

I jumped up and ran to her. Sure enough, there in the box was a stiff, scraggly animal with a pencilpoint snout and a mouth full of pointed teeth. Its eyes were glazed, its tail long and furless. "It must have come in through the broken window in the crawl space," I said, poking it with a stick. "It sure looks dead." Its sharp, tiny teeth were bared in a death grin and it was not breathing. With my wife and our three boys following me, I took the box and dumped what looked like an oversized rat into a hole in the backyard. As we were looking for a shovel to bury the unfortunate creature, up it sprang and away it ran to a hole under the garage. Also springing to life was the phrase "playing possum." We had seen our first opossum and had mistaken it for a large, dead rat with too many teeth.

I still catch one of the possum's red-eyed grandchildren occasionally, foraging for food in the moonlight. I silently wish it well in its hunt and guiltily go to the refrigerator for a late night snack.

The Flight Of The Gulls

In Belmar on Route 35, one must stop when the draw-bridge is up for outgoing or incoming fishing boats. You can do nothing except sit and watch and wait. Turning off the engine, you hear the "*Kweeahah!*" of herring gulls escorting the boats back to the marina. Across from the highway and boat basin is Gull Island, where a group of high-priced and elegant condos now gather. The smell of decaying vegetation, fish, salt water, and creosote fill the air. Above it all is the gulls' elegant flight, full of grace. The gulls wheel and hover as they wait for the bait that a fisherman will throw out, then descend in a flutter of wings and raucous cries to fight over the pieces. The last boat blows its horn as the mast cuts across the highway. Down comes the bridge, on come the engines. The clanging stops and traffic flows again.

Whenever I see a gull, I am reminded of an acquaintance of mine who worked a loader in construction. He told me how, when he took on extra hours moving garbage at the landfill in Toms River, he used to wear earplugs to block out the cries of the gulls that clamored about the yellow loader and the garbage it turned over. "Drove me nuts," he said. "There were hundreds of them. I was going home with the headaches till I

bought the earplugs. Now they don't bother me much." He had seen them at their worst—scavengers and opportunists dependent upon man's garbage for their food.

But gulls are as much a part of the coast as the movement of the waves that their flight accents. Much of the Shore's charm would be lost without them. Consider how they have glided into our stories, paintings, arts and crafts, and many logos for Shore magazines and other businesses. The gulls are at their best at the Shore, where they execute patterns of flight, pearl gray wings against the mussel-blue sky; where they fish for themselves, dipping into a run of herring; or where they rise about fifty feet to let a clam shell fall onto the jetty below, their cries like pulleys on a fishing trawler.

The Dinner Party

Driving over a small wooden bridge in Manasquan, I impetuously turned right toward a salt marsh instead of head-ing for the ocean a few blocks away. The cattails, cord grass, reed grass, and salt marsh bullrushes swayed my imagination. After parking the car on a side street, my wife, children, and I parted the tall grass and rushes. An aviary of squawking birds exploded from the grass and feathered the air with their wings.

We stepped into another world just a few yards from the sidewalk, car, and civilization. There were tiny snails (periwin-kles) feeding on the stalks of the grasses. Lying here and there in mud the color of iodine were long empty razor shells, oyster shells, and hard clam shells. One of the boys whispered, "Wow, look at this!" Scattered on the mud, waving their large claws at us, were about thirty or more fiddler crabs. Fiddlers are as much a part of the salt marshes as the billion-year-old tides that flush it twice a day. The males have one small claw and one large claw; they constantly wave the latter about for defense or communication—hence the name "fiddler." If the large claw is lost or torn off, another grows to take its place. Their eyes are on stalks and can be raised or lowered at will, like periscopes, for a better view of their surroundings. We must have caught them gathering food (particles of dead animals and plants) before the tide came in. What a remarkable sight: thirty or more of these creatures standing on their pointed, jointed legs, claws and eyes raised in the air. We watched for a minute or two before they scurried with a sideways crawl back to their burrows, which aerate the heavy mud of this marsh. When they scurried away, the sound of their insect feet was like the crackling of static electricity. We could barely tell they were there at all after they plugged up their burrows.

The tide was beginning to wash in. Had we arrived two or three minutes later, we would have missed the show.

The Geese

I was never sure what kind of geese they were, but they arrived around Labor Day and never went farther south than Toms River. They stayed near the playground by Pine Beach and on the lawns of the houses across the street. The male was white, the female, gray. I would always see them together, one watching the other feed a few feet away. They mated for life. Coming home along Riverside Drive after a rough day at work, I would slow down to see if they were still there. It somehow calmed me to know they were. And on bright morn-

ings, it cheered my spirits to see the white goose on a deep green lawn.

Sometime in early May, the male was run over by a seventeen-year-old boy. Witnesses said that the car accelerated and swerved into the lane where the goose was crossing. The boy was later caught, fined, and lost his license for three months. Now there are two duck crossing signs with yellow backgrounds and silhouettes of a duck and her three ducklings. The gray goose after several weeks of mournful honking moved up the river to Windy Cove.

A Bit Of Summer Snow

The first time I saw a common egret in its natural surroundings, I was working construction near the fringes of a marsh in Berkeley. When I asked about it, the foreman of the crew said, "I think it's a crane, but I'm not sure what kind. I see a few of them every once in a while, especially in the mornings."

This one stood about three and a half feet high (they are the largest white herons in our area), erect, white, motionless, its stick legs half-hidden in the marsh's water. The early morning sun reflected on its plumage. I could understand why they had been prized by late nineteenth-century hunters, who sold their plumes to the millinery trade for a high price. Partly because of a fashion in women's hats, the common egret nearly became the uncommon egret and by the early 1900s was almost exterminated. But thanks to the Audubon Society stationing wardens in egret rookeries and their advocating laws that forbid the use of egret feathers, the egrets have made a comeback.

I marveled at witnessing a bird of such dazzling white intensity—a bit of summer snow against the tall reeds. Suddenly its long yellow bill parted the water to a flash of fish. The egret rose, the fish glittering in its beak. Slowly flapping its wings, the bird glided away, its stilt legs trailing gracefully.

Nature Versus Man

Recently, I accompanied Walt Doherty, an environmentalist for Toms River Regional Schools, on a class trip to a local cedar swamp. He explained to the children how one day the nature in that area could be gone. "People," he said, "seem to be more interested in their own noise, but if you take a few minutes to stop and listen..." We stopped. We listened. We heard the songs of many different birds. We heard the wind through the Atlantic White Cedar. We heard a splash and a low, heavy croak. We saw the common egret hunting for its prey, its neck taking the shape of a question mark as it swallowed lives. And above us, we heard the sound of a jet.

The intrusion broke the spell. We moved on.

I think about the diversity of life now and the stream of time and realize we are only one of many manifestations of life in that stream. We are fast "conquering" nature, an achievement that we had only dreamed of. In our controlled environments (central heating and air conditioning, neither of which I would give up) we isolate ourselves from the natural world and lose our sensitivity toward other creatures. These "lower forms" of life many times have little to do with us. We fail to acknowledge we are all interconnected, and our world would be less rich and less interesting without them. As Henry Beston writes in *The Outermost House*, his classic about a solitary year spent on a Cape Cod beach, "We need...a wiser, perhaps more mystical concept of animals. They are not brethren, they are not underlings; they are...caught with ourselves in the net of life and time...In a world older and more complete than ours, they move finished and complete, gifted with extensions of the senses we have lost or never attained, living by voices we shall never hear."

First appeared in:
COAST *Magazine, September 1988*
("A Telltale Phrase" is a revision of the essay that originally appeared as "The Possum.")

Paula Kolojeski   "The Marsh In Tuckerton"
18" x 24"   Pastel   1991   Private Collection   Prints Available

Paula Kolojeski   "The Cove"
18" x 24"   Pastel   1993   Private Collection   Prints Available

AUTUMN

September

It is September, and the squirrels are jittery. With the first hint of frost, crickets find their way into houses. Labor Day marks the end of the summer season, and schools open. Traffic thins out, and crowds on the boardwalks dwindle to a cozy few. Winter rental signs pop up. Ragweed and goldenrod proliferate in empty lots. Some days the air is as crisp as a fallen leaf; on others the summer lingers lazily.

In September those seeds of faith planted in May have ripened into Jersey Beefsteak tomatoes. Fresh off the vine and with a little added salt, you can taste the whole summer in a bite. As the nights grow chillier, another blanket is added to the bed. Crickets begin to dwindle down to a precious few. The night sounds and boardwalk crowds diminish. The days of summer innocence are over. Apples are harvested, and school begins.

October

October is pumpkins, plump as full moons; apples, red and golden as the leaves on the trees; and a candle in the jack-o'-lantern to ward off the dark. It's Oktoberfest with brown ale, and Halloween with grotesque-looking trick-or-treaters banging on doors for sweets. The smell of smoke from fireplace chimneys rides the cool wind. A full hunter's moon stalks the sky. A lone fisherman silhouettes the horizon. Nights grow longer.

The air is thinner; a cold wind shakes the leaves from a maple. Frost-loosened, they shower the asphalt streets with gold, yellow, and red. The tree, nearly naked, remains—black bones veining a gray sky. An acrid odor of wet leaves fills the air. The woods are spotted with the red caps of hunters. Children in masks and colorful costumes go from door to door, ringing each bell for treats. A moon-like jack-o'-lantern glowers from the shadows of a porch.

November

November. Autumn's beauty has faded. Political leaflets on the table pile up like leaves on the streets, until someone sweeps them away. On Veterans Day, time to remember soldiers of past wars. The wood is split and stacked, the pantry filled. Along the boardwalk, stands and arcades are boarded up. Gulls and crabs retake the beach.

In November, talk about elections and football games fills the air. Football in America dates back to about 2000 B.C., when the ancient Mayans played a similar game in which they threw a ball through a perpendicular ring high in a stone-walled enclosure. Thanksgiving and family gatherings keep this chilly month warm. Indian corn hangs on the door and rooms fill with the aromas of turkey and pumpkin pie. At the shore, ghostly gulls emerge from a fog bank, then sail back into it and vanish once more.

Adapted from:
COAST Magazine's 1990 and 1991 Jersey Shore Almanac

Dick LaBonté   "September Beach"
20" x 24"   Acrylic   1988   Collection of Frank Allocca   Prints Available

Falling Back

Spring ahead, fall back. Back to school and long pants. Back to soups and coffee, from summer salads and iced tea. To boats in dry-dock from boats in the river. Pull back the ropes that divide the beaches. Take the screens down, put the storm windows up. The stiff brown shoes collecting dust in the closet are brought back, dusted off, and polished, while those expensive running shoes bought at the beginning of summer have long since lost their bounce.

The foreshadowing of autumn came early in August with fall catalogues and back-to-school commercials; in the evening when the weather turned around and people who frequented the boardwalk were few; when a gust of wind shook a flurry of leaves from the locust tree; when the cat jumped into my lap once inside the house. With one deep breath, you could smell autumn in the air.

In late August, spiders built webs large enough to entangle a small boy. Insects whirr, buzz, and hum in the empty lots. For all the insects' multitudinous forms and sounds, it is difficult to believe that most will not survive the first frost. Yet many species have been on earth longer than man. By September, summer is dying, as the contemporary poet, Richard Wilbur, put it in "*Exeunt*":

"All cries are thin and terse;
The field has droned the summer's final mass;
A cricket like a dwindled hearse
Crawls from the dry grass."

After Labor Day, the traffic on the highways thins out and the crowds waiting at restaurants for breakfast or dinner diminish. The terns and gulls claim the shore again. Winter rental signs pop up like goldenrod. But as the shoreline is changing, so is the Shore. More and more summer people are becoming year-round people living in condos by the sea or in new developments with euphemistic names such as "Green Oaks" where, ironically, all the oaks were cut down to create the development.

To me, few things taste as naturally delicious as that first ripe, sun-warmed tomato plucked right off the vine. The Jersey Tomato in its essence. By late September, though, my wife and I are overwhelmed with tomatoes and with trying to save them before the first frost. It becomes no small creative act to find different ways to use them before they rot; from tomato quiche to tomato surprise, ways are found to use them. But I am ready for apples now.

October. Pumpkins and Indian corn in the vegetable bins. Indoors, my wife returns to baking. Brown-sugared, cloved, pineappled and glazed, the aroma of ham permeates each room of the house. In town, store windows are gaudily decorated with macabre scenes and characters. Excitement builds in children who wait as the nights grow colder for their own ghostly transformations. The temperature drops below forty degrees. Only last night, a sudden hailstorm brought down most of the remaining leaves on the neighborhood maple trees. That glorious red and gold wreckage of fall as though some great battle were fought, with many losses. And you can see things you hadn't noticed before: squirrels' nests, the neighbor's covered pool, parts of the garage that need paint and repairs. Tonight the sound is in the trees again. Each gust gives a different inflection, accenting the branches in a special way, creating a language all its own.

First appeared in:
COAST Magazine, September/October 1987

Dawn Hotaling   "Sea-Esta"
22" x 30"   Watercolor   1993
Dr. and Mrs. C. Patton   Prints Available

Stephen Harrington   "Sandy Hook Light, N.J. 1886"
15" x 20"   Composite Ink, Watercolor, and Color Pencil   1996   Prints Available

Ludlow Thorston   "Another Season"
13¹/₂" x 20"   Watercolor   1996   Prints Available

The Apple Farm

In the 60s when most places closed up shortly after Labor Day, and malls were far and few between, visiting an apple farm became part of the fall ritual for my wife, the three boys, and me. As soon as the leaves turned color and spiraled down, we would pile into our Chevy Malibu and drive west to the apple farm in Colt's Neck. Here, the old Jersey, which had earned the nickname "Garden State," still existed. A cornucopia of roadside stands with bins that sagged under the weight of blond husks of corn, plump tomatoes, hefty melons, Buddha-like eggplants, and cobbled hills of apples—a potpourri of dazzling colors much like the leaves themselves, awakened the eyes.

Turning off the highway and into the farm's parking lot, I slid the car into a space near the fringe of the orchard, the tires crunching over gravel. The gnome-like apple trees were a stark contrast to the tall pines we were used to.

Although we called this place "the apple farm," it was no longer a working orchard. But there was enough of the old orchard left to give you a feeling for the spirit of the place. There was a small retail store which sold a wide variety of apples, apple-related products, and other produce. As we entered the store, we could smell the aroma of freshly baked apple pie which filled the cool autumn air.

Besides drinking ten cent Dixie cups of cold apple cider, the boys' favorite thing (and mine as well) was watching the bees. In the far corner of the store there was a glassed-in, cross-section of an active beehive—honeycomb and all. The bees entered through a funnel placed high on the exterior of the store. Vibrant with honeybees, the display would usually have a small group of wide-eyed children also buzzing around. Our boys would stand in awe of the numbers of bees going about their business.

Until I scolded him, my middle son put his face flush with the glass display. Only later did I remember he was highly allergic to bee stings and probably got perverse pleasure from sticking his face right by the hive, secure in the knowledge he could not get stung.

We begrudgingly gave others a chance to discover and enjoy and moved on to the aisle where honey was stocked on shelves. From the various sizes and shapes, we chose a small jar with a chunk of honeycomb left in it—a sweet reminder of where the honey came from.

After we went to the checkout with doughnuts, cider, and honey, I would drive home feeling the day had been well spent. Before we reached the house, we had picked our way through most of the doughnuts and had drunk nearly a half-gallon of apple cider, with my wife and I remarking, after each reach into the bag, how it all tasted so much better in the autumn air.

That night the fascination with bees still buzzed in the boys' heads when I overheard the youngest ask the oldest, "Where do they go in the winter?"

First appeared in:
The Asbury Park Press, September 25, 1993

Theresa Troise Heidel
"Wicker And Coffee"
9" x 12"   Watercolor   1995
Private Collection

Ludlow Thorston   "Morning Rider"
14" x 21"   Watercolor   1980   Prints Available

Dawn Hotaling   "Wheels On The Boards"
18" x 24"   Watercolor   1993   Private Collection   Prints Available

The Legend Of A Tree: Toms River

Leo's Landscaping, located in a two-story wood frame house, looks as if time had passed it by. The house stands on a hill with oak, maple, and pine trees, surrounded by the used car lots, gas stations, and fast-food restaurants of the six-lane Route 37. Its screens are patched but in place, its red paint faded but not yet peeling, and its roof, though intact, has shingles missing. The rain gutters, here and there, overflow with pine needles and leaves.

Leo had called the sign shop where I work, saying, "With this increased traffic, my house needs a sign that'll catch drivers' attention." So Ray and I drove out to see what we might do for him. Because we picked up speed after the last traffic light, we nearly missed the place. Turning sharply, I navigated the van up the dirt driveway and stopped in a billow of dust, next to a great tree stump that was spiraled with rings. In the yard near the driveway, several pine trees eclipsed the sun, leaving our van in a pool of deep shade.

When we knocked on the weathered screen door, its rusty hinges rattled. Behind us, traffic whooshed loudly; inside the house, nothing seemed to move. We knocked even louder before going back to the van; Ray was swearing about the heat and lost time.

As I turned the ignition key, a man in his late 60s opened the screen door. This, presumably, was Leo. I cut the engine as he ambled over to the van. "It's difficult to hear anything on that porch with all these cars swooshing by," he said. "Come on, I'll show you what I'm looking for."

Ray and I got out and followed him down to the sign, which was between two four-by-four posts about ten yards from the road. Leo, raising his voice above the methodical hum of traffic, gave us the details of what he wanted on the sign. As we talked, the constant breeze from the cars whipped our hair and ballooned our shirts. Mesmerized by the flow of trucks, cars, vans, and RVs, I said, "I remember when this was a two-lane highway."

Leo laughed. "I've been here forty-five years, and I remember when it was a gravel road."

We stood just outside the shade of the pines. Ray took notes on how the sign should look. I tried to picture Route 37 as a gravel road, then gave up when the traffic light turned green and, like a dam, released the next rush of cars.

Working my way back into the shade, I said, "You have some magnificent trees here."

"I had a beautiful Norway maple out front by the porch," Leo said. "People used to stop and stare at it. The stump is still there. I couldn't pull it out because of the damned root system; I would've had to tear up the whole front yard and God knows what else."

"What happened?" I asked.

"When they added lanes to Route 37, they took about six feet from my front yard and pruned some of the maple's crown, so it wouldn't interfere with the telephone wire. About a year later, a telephone worker in a cherry picker comes and saws off large chunks of the maple's branches nearest the highway. He said they were doing it so they wouldn't have to come back every year to prune. Well, then, I had a one-sided tree. That's not a hell of a good advertisement for a landscaping business, I thought. So me and a couple of my men cut it down—even though it broke my heart to do it. The tree was filled with so much water, we had to wipe the sawblade dry after each cut. It took three men to carry one three-foot piece."

The following summer, he said, he couldn't figure out why it was almost twenty-degrees hotter on the porch. Then it dawned on him that his Norway maple had made the difference. "That tree was the best damn air-conditioner around. It kept the noise of the cars down too."

Ray finished the sketch of the sign and told Leo we'd get back to him. When we returned to the van, I took one last look at the stump. Its great girth had numerous dark and light rings that varied in thickness—a legend of its many years. I pictured the Norway maple as it must have been: a castle of deep green leaves, symmetrical and lofty with birds, squirrels, and cicadas. On clear days, its hundreds of leaves would be a dazzling green against a radiant sky. When windy, the leaves would rustle and sound like rain, and in fall they'd flush with the season's colors: bright red, orange and yellow, a wonderous show that made people stop and stare.

With a wave, we left Leo and drove west on Route 37. We passed a new fast-food place with "Grand Opening" buntings draped around its eaves. Farther down the highway, workers in their yellow hard-hats were laying out another strip mall. Under a once branchy sky, black clouds of diesel smoke hung above bulldozers, loaders, and huge dump trunks. Lying by their craters, giant trees bared their amputated roots.

While waiting at a red light, I looked through the heat-wrinkled air above the line of traffic and thought about Shel Silverstein's book, *The Giving Tree* in which a tree loves a little boy. As the boy grows up, he takes more and more from the tree: shade, leaves, apples, branches for a house, and, in middle age, wood for a boat. When the middle-age man returns an old man after his many voyages, all that's left of the tree is a stump. The old man sits on it and is, finally, wise enough to appreciate what the tree has given him.

Squinting at the construction site through waves of exhaust fumes and heat, I thought for an instant I caught the faint outline of children running and playing in shade. Then Ray called out, "Frank! The light's green!" and I drove on.

First appeared in:
COAST *Magazine, September,* 1989
Anthologized in:
Shore Stories, 1998

Dawn Hotaling   "Patten Avenue Boats"
22" x 30"   Watercolor   1994   Private Collection   Prints Available

Theresa Troise Heidel   "St. Catharine's, Christmastime"
10" x 9"   Watercolor and Gouache   1994   Private Collection

CHRISTMAS

December

The first snowfall usually comes in December. Hanukkah is celebrated this month, as the menorah is lit one branch at a time. People yearn for a white Christmas—a rarity—as families get together. Santa Clauses appear to be everywhere, along with wreathes, poinsettias, and bells. The tree is picked out, brought home, and placed in the corner—a triangle of green in mid-winter. Mistletoe hangs in doorways, and celebration hangs in the carols that chorus the night with white breath.

Nights are at their longest this month, and chimney smoke rides the cold air. There is magic in the first snow of winter; it transforms the landscape and alters the vision. December is exhilarating with its holiday celebrations of Hanukkah and Christmas. Evergreen trees and red-leaved poinsettias add to the season's color; Eggnog with cinnamon and nutmeg sprinklings add to the taste. The sound of December is bells and carolers ringing and singing brightly in the cold, dark air.

Adapted from:
COAST Magazine's 1990 and 1991 Jersey Shore Almanac

Theresa Troise Heidel   "St. Catharine's At Christmas"
9" x 11"   Watercolor and Gouache   1996

The Legacy

The Christmas holidays are forever linked in my memories with my uncle and the Lionel train set he started for me. When I was eight, I opened the first gift package under the bubbling lights of the Christmas tree. Dense with mystery, the box felt heavier than a metal bank full of pennies. In went my hands and out came a black beauty, a locomotive with six silver wheels, each reflecting the lights of the tree. Other packages contained a tender car, a small transformer, and enough "027" gauge track to encircle the Christmas tree. I remember my aunt cautioning my uncle, "Do you really think he's old enough to have such an expensive gift?" My uncle, always calm, replied, "Of course, he is." He then instructed me on how to set up the transformer, warning me to keep my fingers away from the live wires. My aunt's countenance changed from concern to admiration as she offered her brother some eggnog. She remained unsure about, "that wild boy" but she trusted her brother. So did I.

The Christmas tree did not burn down that year or in the many years that followed. My aunt's worst fears diminished as my uncle continued to give me a car a year: a gondola car, boxcar, tank car, coal car.... I *became* the great steam locomotive, pulling freight under tunnels of chairs and bridges of blocks, steaming past the tall forest of the Christmas tree wrapped in cotton snow, wailing like a coonhound in the night. The sharp, warm smell of electricity filled my nostrils, and faraway names rattled my imagination: Erie, Wabash, Rio Grande, Santa Fe...

One Christmas, dressed in his red suit and white beard, my uncle came in out of the night, stomped the snow off his black boots, shook his pillowy belly, and HO-HO-HOed the children awake. From his bulky sack, he began distributing presents. The thin paper on mine felt cold with melting snow. Staying a short while, he disappeared only to reappear later as my disappointed uncle who stuck to his story of missing Santa's visit. That Christmas, I received the car I had dreamed about night after night, anticipating all the uses it would fulfill in my railroad. Opening the dream, the automatic, refrigerated milk car emerged, white as the milk it delivered, with seven silver milk cans. I loaded the cans into the hinged roof hatch, pulled the car onto the remote control track, and endlessly buzzed the little man to deliver milk. Watching him was like watching the cuckoo pop out of the clock without having to wait an hour to catch it. I reloaded so often that my thumb showed the dark indentations of milk cans.

The last car I received from my uncle, before he and his family moved to Ohio, was a red caboose. Although my uncle occasionally wrote and visited afterwards, Christmas was never quite the same. The company he worked for selling lamps had laid off a number of their salesmen, so he had to work longer hours and travel farther. At the few family Christmases he came to, he looked tired as a tombstone. I was growing older, too, and becoming interested in girls and in competing for track. Sometimes though, I'd daydream about catching a boxcar on a long freight train, riding to Ohio and showing up in Cleveland on his doorstep. He'd hug me tight and wouldn't worry about how I got there. We'd sit and reminisce about past Christmases, about trains, and our family. He'd offer eggnog. But it was not to be.

When "Silent Night" and "Silver Bells" drift through the air of every mall and every department store raises its clockwork Santa, I make my way through the crowd to the model railroad display. There, I catch a whiff of the old electricity and feel the warm rush of past Christmases...the Lionel days of my childhood. But I especially remember my uncle and the world he opened up for me.

First appeared in:
COAST Magazine, November/December 1987
Reminisce (Extra), December 1994 (appeared titled as "His Holidays Were Lionel Days")
Anthologized in:
First Light: Poems, Stories and Essays of the Winter Holiday Season, 1997

Theresa Troise Heidel   "Victorian Christmas, Spring Lake"
9" x 12"   Watercolor and Gouache   1996

Dick LaBonté   "Christmas In Bay Head"
20" x 24"   Acrylic   1992   Collection of Artist   Prints Available

Assembling The Toys

On that Christmas Eve my younger brother, discharged two months earlier from the army after four years of service in Korea, came to live with us temporarily in a two-bedroom apartment in Bradley Beach. Now twenty-one, he was working at the Gulf station pumping gas, doing a little mechanical work, and looking at the want ads in the New York City papers.

I picked him up with all his baggage at the train station just as fine, powdery flakes of snow started to fall. Driving back to Bradley Beach, our mood was buoyant. Our battered '59 Buick coasted along the road, trailing white streamers of snow. We drove past lawns of Santas and sleighs pulled by bright reindeer; the ornaments seemed to urge us on, strengthening our desire for Christmas cheer.

Arriving at the three-story brick building where I lived with my wife and three sons, we saw four-year-old Steven looking out the lighted kitchen window. From the church across the street, all lit up for midnight mass, the bells rang, "O Come, All Ye Faithful." Steven liked to look at the Madonna in front of the church; he had heard from his brothers that the statue could move and ever since had kept a vigil. But that night, the Madonna could have done a small jig and Steven would not have noticed; he was watching for his Uncle Louie.

My wife greeted us at the door, the children jumping up and down behind her. Seven-year-old Mike, the oldest, yelled, "Uncle Louie, we get to open one present before we go to bed."

"Yeah, and it's probably clothes," said Alan, who, though two years younger than Mike, already had a pragmatic attitude; he knew that for the last few years the first gift had been Christmas pajamas. Steven didn't say anything as he tore his package open. He dumped its contents on the floor: a pair of bright red pajamas with feet. Alan received the same, only larger. Mike's had snowflake designs and no feet but inside his box he found a pair of red socks. "We get to open the real gifts tomorrow morning," he said.

"Yeah, the toys," Alan said with a grin.

After changing into their Christmas pajamas, the boys went to bed whining, "But we want to see Uncle Louie!"

"You have," my wife replied. "He'll still be here tomorrow."

After goodnight kisses and the closing of the bedroom door, the real work began, assembling the toys: three tricycles of various sizes and one two-story parking garage and gas station. My brother, riveted by the inner mysteries of machines, was chosen to assemble the gifts. My wife, who could make uncanny sense out of the most abstruse language, read the directions. I, the mechanically disinclined, got to hand my brother the tools, an easy job since we had only two, a regular screwdriver and a claw hammer.

"Where are your wrenches?" my brother asked.

I went to the kitchen and dug through the small tool drawer which held assorted nails, screws, thumbtacks, rolls of string, old extension cords, safety pins, and a miscellany of unidentified metal objects. I returned with a pair of all-purpose vise grips. "Where's your Phillips screwdriver?" my brother asked. Barb responded by rummaging through her pocketbook and pulling out a nail file.

"Don't you people have any tools?" Louie asked before resignedly plunging into the task of assembling the toys.

He made it through the tricycles with hardly an audible "Damn," but the two-story tin parking garage/gas station eroded his composure and drew blood as one insert sliced his thumb. "No, I'm all right," he said to my wife who was about to get him a band-aid. "What time is it?"

"Four a.m.," my wife said. "The kids will be up soon. They always wake up on Christmas with the first light."

"Hey, I fix cars for a living; I'm a professional," my brother said. "No toy ever got the best of me!" And then we all plunged in, attacking the garage with true Christmas spirit, each of us intent on our specific tasks.

"Are you sure that's how the directions read?"

"Here, see for yourself."

"Well then, we're missing a part."

"Here—Frank is sitting on it."

"What time is it?"

"Quarter after five."

"I have slot A. Where's tab B?"

"Don't look at me. I'm not sitting on it."

"Here's tab D. Is that close enough?"

"I'm going to make some coffee. Frank, give me back the can opener."

"But we may need it."

"Give me those directions again."

"What time is it?"

"Six o'clock."

"Frank, hand me that nail file."

And so it went. My brother inserted the final tab into the final slot just as the windowpanes were turning rosy with light. As we were thanking him profusely, he let out a sigh and collapsed onto the couch with his bandaged thumb, muttering about directions and Japanese toys.

As he started to fall asleep, the boys stampeded down the stairs and jumped onto Uncle Louie's lap.

"Uncle Louie, Uncle Louie, look what Santa left us! Gee, you look tired. What happened to your finger?"

"Huh?" my brother mumbled groggily. He straightened out his glasses and looked at his thumb as though it didn't belong to him. "Oh that." He attempted to get up but fell back onto the sofa again. "I think I cut it at the gas station." He mumbled a Merry Christmas or at least that's what I thought he said.

Later, as we three sipped freshly brewed coffee and glanced out at the first churchgoers decked in their Christmas best, the bells rang out *"Joy To The World,"* and the children, wildly pedaling in small circles, jingled the bells of their tricycles.

First appeared in:
COAST *Magazine, December 1988*
Down Memory Lane, December/January 1993
Anthologized in:
First Light: Poems, Stories and Essays of the Winter Holiday Season, 1997

Theresa Troise Heidel
"Ocean Grove Christmas"
10" x 10"   Watercolor   1998

Ludlow Thorston   "Change In The Weather"
12" x 18½"   Watercolor   1997   Prints Available

The Gift Of The Tree

When an artist friend invited me to her home in Rumson for the lighting of her Christmas tree, it did not seem as though it would be a rousing event. My friend, though, is of German descent and lights her tree the way people did before electricity—with candles.

She had saved Christmas balls which had been passed down through generations. Some of the balls dated back to 1905 and had tallow still hardened on them from past lightings. The oldest of these were made of thin-blown glass with a silvery finish; on some, tallow had hardened and then dropped off, leaving patches of discoloration.

In the old days, my friend told me, back when nights were much deeper, her family would gather around the tree for the first lighting. Oranges, a rarity in the winter, would dangle from the branches, along with apples and little sacks of potpourri which emitted a cinnamon aroma that blended with the spicy balsam of the tree. Clipped at the tip of the branches would be tallow candles, each in a spring clip holder with a cup to catch the droppings.

With a long matchstick, her father lit each wick, as the tallow sputtered and spit. Glowing in the candlelight with the peacefulness of the gathering, the family sang choruses from "*The First Noel*," "*O Holy Night*," "*Tannenbaum*," and "*Silent Night*." Later, there was a second lighting during which they would open their gifts.

And so it was that my friend aspired to pass on to her children and share with her friends the lighting of the tree. Arriving in Rumson that night, I entered the main room of her art studio; a pot-bellied stove was set on a square of bricks in the room's center, and several of her paintings were framed along the walls. The tree, off in a far corner, seemed no different than most. It was decorated much as my friend described her parents' tree. She chose a well-tapered fir, having no branches above any candle flame, and the effect was that of a candelabrum.

Slowly the guests trickled in. When everyone was relaxed with his or her food and drink, the lights dimmed. My friend lit a long matchstick and began slowly to light the candles. After the first few, the electricity was switched off. Patterns of shadow and light entwined on the gathered faces, and the room seemed transfigured with an ethereal glow. All eyes were focused on the tree.

The presence of the evergreen emerged from the darkness. The conversation grew hushed and time flickered like flames. I thought of prehistoric man gathered around campfires in shadowy caves, of medieval cathedrals and bonfires, of Martin Luther, the Protestant reformer, who, upon returning home from a walk in the snow-silent woods, felt spiritually lifted up by the beauty of thousands of glittering stars in the sky. He could not describe in words to his wife and children the wonder of what he had experienced. Cutting down a small fir in his garden, he set up the tree in his nursery and lighted the branches with candles to convey the glory of the heavens that was revealed to him that cold winter's night. I thought of the ending of the old year and the evergreen hopes of the new one.

Quietly at first, then with growing spirit, the singing of the Christmas carols began. It started with "The First Noel," reached a crescendo with "Joy To The World," and a diminuendo with "Silent Night," the voices trailing off into the quietness of candles. This all transpired in a space of twenty minutes. Finally, the candles were extinguished, the flames snuffed one by one. But their light prevailed in each of the faces around the tree.

First appeared in:
COAST Magazine, December 1988

Theresa Troise Heidel   "Avon Pavilion On A Misty Day"
8" x 10"   Watercolor   1995   Private Collection

Theresa Troise Heidel   "Asbury Remembered"
18" x 24"   Watercolor and Gouache   1990   Private Collection   Prints Available

Theresa Troise Heidel

"Neptune And Seashell"
8" x 11"   Watercolor   1997
Private Collection

"Carousel Top"
15" x 19"   Watercolor   1997

"Lantern And Dolphins"
9" x 10"   Watercolor   1995
Private Collection

Sally

I was never one for artificial trees but my stepmother bought one once. Aluminum and small enough to fit on her stereo, it had a snow-sprayed, cardboard color wheel with red, green, blue, and yellow cellophane that rotated when plugged in. She had her reasons for buying it: her apartment was small and on the second floor; her two boys had moved out years before; it was cheaper, requiring no expensive decorations; it was easier to store and it was durable. She didn't have to struggle with putting it up, with decorating it, or with taking it down when January showed its new face. These were all sound reasons, and I did not begrudge them. She thought it was beautiful. Secretly, though, I named it "Disco Tree" because of its rotating, color wheel which cast spinning, colored lights on the ceiling, creating a dome-ball effect.

Once, while visiting my stepmother before the holidays, she fell asleep on the couch watching (for the 20th time) the uncolorized, 1947 version of "*Miracle on 34th Street.*" I covered her with an afghan, turned off the TV, and stared at the aluminum tree. Its silvery strips were moving up and down in a current of warm air which came from the heating vent. As the color wheel rotated, the whole room took on the lighting of a dance floor with baubles of light like planets circling ceiling and walls.

My stepmother loved to go to dances in starlit ballrooms, and even into her late sixties she outshone many twenty-year olds. She was 5'1", quite busty and hippy—a body, it would seem, more suited to watching TV—but once out on the dance floor, smiling and singing along with the music, she was light and graceful. Her body energized and transmitted her happiness to almost everyone she danced with, young and old.

When she was four or five, her father used to take her to weddings. She would dance for the bride and groom who would clear a table for her. The people would throw pennies, and her father would keep the pennies in a bag for her to buy Christmas gifts. She had five sisters and three brothers and she loved children. She taught her brothers how to lead and steps to the different dances. Before her father came home from work, she would teach her younger sisters who begged, "Balla, *balla con mia!*" (Dance, dance with me!). In the 20s, she would Charleston, shimmy, flea hop, and Chicago. In the 60s, she would mambo, cha-cha, tango, Lindy, and twist. She would crash parties and weddings, mingle with the guests, pluck the wallflowers from their walls and have them up and dancing and enjoying it. "I had a ball," she'd say, fanning herself. She would dance with men, other women, children, and even by herself to music on a jukebox. "Dancing is my life," she'd say.

Once, when my father was making his eggs, a song she liked was playing on the radio. She turned up the volume, turned off the burner, grabbed my father and said, "Let's cut a rug, kid." He muttered, "Cheeze, Sally, you're crazy!" But a minute later, he was smiling and dancing the Lindy as the pans on the kitchen shelf rattled.

My stepmother has arthritis and, at 79, doesn't dance much anymore. Over the years, she and I have had our differences—when to eat, who to marry, where to live, among others. When I looked at her sleeping under the wheeling lights of that first aluminum tree, I thought of her dancing through all those years and the differences blend into a warm blur.

That night I dreamed of a small, dancing tree with bright lights and a circle of smiling children gathered around it. They had their arms stretched out in front of them and were calling out in various tongues, "Dance, dance with me!"

First appeared in:
Footwork: The Paterson Literary Review, Issue 23, 1993
Anthologized in:
Identity Lessons: Learning American Style: An Anthology Of Contemporary Writing, 1999

Ludlow Thorston   "Carrousel"
2¹/₄" x 9³/₄"   Watercolor   1980   Prints Available

Paula Kolojeski   "Asbury Park Carousel"
18" x 24"   Pastel   1992   Private Collection

Dawn Hotaling   "Palace Amusements"
20" x 28"   Watercolor   1993   Private Collection   Prints Available

Old Gray

The first winter Barb and I moved to Pine Beach, it was so cold that the Toms River froze. During that winter, Barb began feeding the birds. She would toss handfuls of wild birdseed, cracked corn, sunflower seeds, and bread into our backyard. Within minutes, the call went out as sparrows, starlings, mourning doves, cardinals, blue jays, and finches swept down from the trees. Their blacks, browns, golds, blues, and reds created a striking effect against the snow.

Among the birds there were always the gray tree squirrels; twitchy, quick, and chattery, their presence would immediately scatter the birds. At first, we were simply annoyed at their intrusion and naively thought to scare them away. We shouted and made wild movements toward the boldest of the squirrels. He would stay till we were almost within reach, then, turn and dash up a pine tree and wait on the opposite side of the trunk. We would withdraw to the house, the birds would flutter down to feed again, and the squirrels would return. It seemed a losing battle.

In the years following, we bought a number of what we believed would be squirrel-proof birdfeeders. We fastened one on a clothesline strung about four feet above the ground between a locust tree and a pine. One afternoon we discovered the clothesline lying like a slack snake on the ground. We spotted Old Gray—we now had a name for him—munching on spilled sunflower seeds. Examining the snapped clothesline, we discovered it had been chewed in two. Old Gray had applied an old skill to a new situation.

Another time, we bought a birdfeeder that looked like a birdhouse; made of clear plastic with a detachable roof, it had seed troughs running along its four sides. We fastened the roof with electrical tape and put the feeder on a pole about four-foot high which stood well away from the trees. After a few days, we saw more spilled seeds on the ground than there should have been. Though we could not figure out how he did it, we suspected Old Gray. Then, one day, while looking out the window, we caught him making an incredibly acrobatic leap from the grape arbor on the garage to the feeder about seven feet away. Seeds fell to the ground. The pole and feeder wobbled precariously with Old Gray perched on top.

One morning, not long after that, we saw the feeder wiggling by itself and the roof with shredded tape upside down on the ground. Then, from the middle of the feeder, up popped Gray with his bushy, question mark tail and pointy head, his forepaws to his mouth as he munched on a seed. We had to laugh. He looked like a long-time resident of the place.

We resigned ourselves to the inevitable; whatever we did, Old Gray and the other squirrels were going to get their share of seeds and more. Occasionally, our black cat, Shadow, would chase the squirrels onto their respective perches. Old Gray would take up his favorite position on a half-dead limb of the locust tree that overlooks our backyard door. His tail furiously twitching, he would look down at Shadow and scold him with a *chirr-chirr-chirr* while chattering his teeth.

For years, Old Gray and I tolerated each other and somehow were bound to each other by that toleration. It wasn't until another snowy winter that my toleration slipped into a deeper feeling. Barb was preparing one of those festive, holiday "I'll-begin-my-diet-tomorrow" meals for family and relatives. She began laying the groundwork for this meal the night before. The air in the kitchen was laced with the garlicky scent of meatballs frying. On the stove, huge pots bubbled and steamed like active volcanoes. Ladles and large spoons coated with thick red sauce lay on the counter next to the stove.

The next morning, the kitchen counters were filled with platters of various sizes and bowls of food, all wrapped in aluminum foil. It looked like a silver mountain range. The aroma of baked ham—brown-sugared, cloved, pineapply, and glazed—permeated the house.

Outside, the thermometer read twenty-five degrees Fahrenheit. A strong wind bent the pines, the kind of wind that whitecaps the river and makes the temperature seem as though it were ten below zero. The snow was already a few inches deep when guests began arriving.

During dinner, over the din of plates clattering, glasses clinking, Uncle Tony laughing too loudly, and Aunt Marie raising her voice to make a point to Uncle Bob about her latest cause (Save The Pigeons), Barb thought she heard rattling on the back screen door. She got up from the table and looked out the kitchen window. No one was there. She returned to her dinner. Again, the rattling. This time I heard it too.

We both went to the back door and opened it. Barb saw tiny footprints in the snow leading to the locust tree. Looking up, we saw Old Gray, bushy tail billowing in the wind, standing on his perch next to a lump of snow. His crow-black eyes fixed on us. He sat on his haunches, his forepaws in a prayer-like position. Having been preoccupied with preparing the meal, Barb forgot to put seed in the feeder. She went back into the kitchen as Old Gray shook the snowflakes off his fur and came down from the tree to the door and actually waited on the steps. I believe he might have come in had I invited him.

Barb came back with some fresh bread and a suet ball studded with sunflower seeds. Gingerly, he took the bread from her hand, put it in his mouth, turned and bounded a few feet away to the base of the locust tree. There he stopped, sat up and nibbled on the bread as he watched us. Barb left the suet ball on the steps. Closing the door, I stood and observed a while at the window. Gray dropped his bread and loped over to the suet ball where he meticulously picked off the sunflower seeds, leaving the suet for the birds.

I went back to the dining room where a myriad of smells wafted above the heaps of food on the table—candied yams, pickled beets, corn, green beans, and spritzels, mashed potatoes, and hot buttered muffins. After the meal came the desserts: pumpkin and pecan pies, chocolate-covered cherries, mints, oranges, apples, and nuts. As I cracked open a walnut, Old Gray streaked through my mind. It was still snowing and I pictured him curled up in some hollow tree, munching on a seed. Later in the evening, the aunts, uncles, and cousins would be exchanging and opening presents. I had received mine earlier with Barbara's gift to Old Gray who changed from being an annoyance and a nuisance to joining our extended family. Somehow our house seemed warmer.

First appeared in:
COAST *Magazine, December* 1989

Margaret Tourison Berndt
"Ducks In A Row"
48" x 36"   Acrylic   1995
Collection of Katherine and Philip Dougall

Theresa Troise Heidel   "Bridge On Shark River, Belmar, N.J."
8" x 12"   Watercolor   1994   Private Collection

Theresa Troise Heidel

"Shark River, Early Evening"
12" x 16"   Watercolor   1997
Private Collection

"Bridge On Shark River,
Avon-by-the-Sea, N.J."
10" x 14"   Watercolor and Gouache
1996   Private Collection

POETRY

Theresa Troise Heidel   "Belmar Gazebo"
8" x 12"   Watercolor   1995

Sea Oats: Island Beach State Park

The great yellow eye of the sun is lost
in the sea oats that anchor this sand.
Nights grow longer, colder by degrees, and frost
begins to feather vines of grapes and pumpkins—
the unpicked harvest, star-crossed.
An icy wind rustles the dune's dry stalks
and stars begin to shiver in the deepening dark.

Twilight Lake

reflects this Bay Head morning
smooth and bright as the mute swan
that floats out from
the rushes, reeds, and cattails.
Ducks circle the lake and plash
down, breaking the reflection.
They paddle to where a young
couple and their small girl throw
bits of white bread on the grass.
A little lake of gulls, doves,
mallards, and geese shapes about them,
while damselflies and darning needles
hover and dart above the fragrant
water lilies. Across the avenue,
Victorians and cedarshake cottages
hold vigil over this sanctuary. An artist
sets up his white canvas and begins
to paint what is there, what is not.

Seascape: Manasquan, NJ

Wet shells glitter the beach
splinters of light needling sand and eye.
Gulls sail on waves of breeze
        skim rocks' mussels and glide
                preying over crosses of masts.
To life that tunes its pitch to scales of waves,
the slow sea whistles the rhythm of sun and moon.
        Fiddlers step through sand in time
and broken crabs' claws lie;
between the charred drift they tumbled
        up to shore, teeth to sand.
Brittle as fall's last leaves,
shroud in rags of seaweed,
        rich in decay,
the forests of the sea's dead
lying under indifferent gulls—
wet shells glittering the beach.

Reign Of Fire: Asbury Park

From the telephone wires,
sparrows' voices pierce the ear.
The clouds are not all vapor
that pass over here; a town
away, a city is burning. There's smoke
from windows, fire on streets—
black clouds contain a man's
skin—rats in cellars are sizzling,
the old beams burning, waterbugs
bubbling, hissing into flames,
the tar roofs boiling, and
no one can get in or out.

Horns jamming, siren blues
wailing, Fourth of July, we're burning
the wooden-storied buildings,
the facades we supported so long
so long, good-bye. Good-bye
to the other side of the tracks;
we're railing our way over. Glass
in streets glitters our dreams.

A fireman hoses the blaze.
From boarded buildings, spray-paint
words flare at a phalanx of police.
A black woman looks for her son—
there are flames in his mouth, hell
in the cage of his ribs.

River Watch

Toms River, NJ

The halyards on aluminum masts begin
chinging like little buoys.
Upriver a speedboat buzzes open
a white scar. Sailboats waggle
their masts as though anticipating a wind.
Low lapping sounds reach the bank;
deposit crab claws, driftwood, pebbles, then leave;
return with weeds, shells; leave
with flowers; return. Leave. The sailboats are still,
the river metallic
in scales of light—a chain of mail.
On the river's bank, all
the houses scintilla the sun, their windows
shrill with light. The brilliance
recedes. The river purls into twilight
and the dark bay of the ocean.

Point Pleasant Beach

Late October. Xylophone
snowfences diagonal
the sand. Lath after
lath, they cast a shadow
clock, where gulls reclaim
mussels. Martell's Sea Breeze rolls
down its door to summer, while
a skein of pale geese
traces the shoreline.
On the south end of the boardwalk
more condos rise. Beyond,
a Victorian turret
faint in sea mist.

Last Stop

Bay Head Station. End
of the line for New Jersey
Transit. Only a thousand
three hundred residents
year round. Katherine
Hepburn lived here.
The bygone Lorraine movie house
is specialty shops now, but
All Saints Episcopal and
the Yacht Club endure
into the new millennium.
The salt-white clock tower
and cross of the Sacred Heart Church
shine over Route 35 blacktop.
Sea and wind sculpt
this beach of high dunes,
and tourists still come
to sun and praise.
The Northern Cross takes
its place in the August sky
just as it did when
the Lenni-Lenape looked up
from their longhouses
and all things
possessed a spirit.

Laird's Applejack (Monmouth, N. J., 1698)

I am drinking New Jersey's oldest brandy—
America's oldest brandy. It's George
Washington who asked for the recipe
around 1760—and got it.
It's the Virginia Colony
he introduced it to & here am I
drinking that brandy with its "subtle hint
of apple" & all the orchards of this
fast, diminishing Garden State. It warms
my brain & I think of the icy
Delaware in December 1776
& the Battle of Trenton—a turning point.
I am in my newly built town house watching
three survivors struggle across the Kalahari
Desert on the VCR. My wife sits next to me
on the double recliner sofa. She makes out
the winter bills & there is a fire
in my belly, but it's not the brandy.

Tomorrow I will go out to see
the tiny, vandalized graveyard
& 350 year old white oak
our builder told his dozer man
not to knock down or he would lose
his job. There I will touch wrinkled bark
older than the brandy & history that touched me.

Jersey Shore Vacation Again

The same "Don't Wanna Go
Home" crowds walk the boards,
breathe in hot dogs, suntan lotion,
saltwater taffy, creosote. At night
bands vibrate floors with fifties
revival songs, hard rock, country.
Bartender rings up change
to the clink of empty bottles.
In the corner, the silent TV.
Morning surf roar. Water and air.
Breathe in crystals of mica-glinting
sea, till salt speckles lungs
and mind becomes clear
as a gull's sweep over the jetty.
It's the summer solstice.
Step up. Take a chance.

The Fishermen:
Island Beach State Park

The fishermen—ocean wise—watch.   Gripped
by the Atlantic, they stand   casting   planting
their poles   against the horizon.   The surf
hissing bright   breaks   coiling around
their boots.   Sundown.   Moonrise.   The beach
a lunar desert. Hooking into the dark,
they light their driftwood fires.   Wait.
The moon, a phosphorescent glow, hosts their forms.
Hours later, turning to sea again, sun
forsythias the horizon.   On scales
of light, fishermen's pitched figures,
like notes, inherit the music
of this place.   A smell of salt   crystals   the air.

Island Beach State Park

Once over the high dunes
a rush of light, an expanse of space.
Loose curves of tideline, arcs of gulls
and pale horizon replace
buildings' hard angles,
grids of blocks. Here, waves glitter
a thousand small suns. A herring gull
Kweeeah-ahs like a rusty pulley,
while an osprey whistles its *you you you*
circling toward bayside cedars.
A hollow boom echoes up and
down the shore, a white hiss
of foam—the mantra of the sea.

The long rhythm of the surf in my ears, I step
into the necklace of the tideline:
the clatter and crunch of periwinkles,
scallops, jackknife clams; bits of sponge,
moon shells, a mermaid's purse;
even a gull's skull picked clean by beetles,
its sharp, yellow beak still menacing.
The only prints along wet, darkened sand
are the cuneiform tracks of gulls
and my own. Here, under a sky
the color of salt, my aloneness
grows exquisite as beach glass:
turquoise, amber, emerald...

Fishermen

Walking from the restaurant, I wander onto
the beach, meeting one by one the fishermen
silhouetted on splinters of sunset. The reels spin out
their lines; draw me into the web
of their universe. It's darker now, darker
than the shadows of those souls when I first spied them.
Going from fisherman to fisherman, I listen
to each tale of the one they reeled in, or the one
that's still out there; of how their grandfathers fished
before them and their fathers. I move farther and farther
from that lighted restaurant. I feel the white nylon
cord slip beneath the sea, grow taut. I see
the metal barb sharp as a new moon.
Mesmerized by driftwood fires, stars, ocean,
I hook into their lives. A thousand lifetimes ago.

City Girls At Seaside Heights

They will come again this summer, bare-legged
girls with boys under their asses,
to try and grab a piece
of the sun. The rum in their tropical
drinks will blossom their cheeks, their dreams
grow verdant in August; they will move
their tans over the dark cracks
of the boardwalk, to the rhythm of steel
vibrations on dance floors or behind
the shine of dark glasses and ice-white
smiles. Like salmon running upstream
to spawn, they will flash their tails,
till all their bubble and boil expends
itself leaving plastic bottles and reeds
of straws—the bones of their dollars
and time dissolving on the sand.

On The Boardwalk At Point Pleasant Beach

A monopoly of summer
cottages lines the north boardwalk
then gives way to gift shops, food stands,
and arcades widening into the heart
of Jenkinson's Pavilion, where games
crackle with light and the perpetual chatter
of push-button weapons blasting cosmic
targets. A wispy, sweet smell of cotton
candy slips through the spicy aroma
of sausage and peppers. Some afternoons,
I sit on a bench near the railing and read
sea poems from a pocket anthology, while the sea
whispers for me to look up and listen
to the real thing. Later, the sand blooms
with beach umbrellas and oil-shined bathers
who rediscover the Jersey shore.
I play Skee-Ball and pinball in arcades
where machines blink away
my quarters in a twinkle of lights.
Or, under a thatched umbrella at Martell's
Tiki Bar, I listen to reggae of No Discipline,
tinkle of ice, laughter of crowd, and hiss-boom
of sea. The waitress serves a parasoled drink.
Dusk deepens. The crowd swells and families sail
into the night, their pockets laden with change.
Inside the boardwalk's new aquarium,
exotic fish glide back and forth
as stars go silently over the ocean.

The Galleon

She sails—her leaves
billowing in the wind turn up
white as the bellies of fish. Her masts
forking into twigs, crows
nesting on her timbers, the rigging
of vines swaggers in gusts of salt-wind.
A dome of thunder looms
over her. Waves of wind
break over her boughs. Seasoned
in weathers, she groans. The hold
of roots swells with water. Her sides
split yellow-white with cracks
of lightning—the living scamper and fly
to abandon her.   Morning.   We find
black wreckage of branches strewn
over a sea of grass and hear
breezes fluttering the torn sails.

Tail End, Summer

Fireballs of sirens spin light off
buildings, trees, crowds; people
with robes, bare feet, people
I have not seen before on the street
come watch. A red pulsating beat,
the ambulance, doors agape, idles.
"What's happening?" "I don't know,
but I think..." Two Puerto Ricans,
a white, knees going chest-high, sprint
past, bellowing. Now half the town is out.
A bull of a man in blue
horns the crowd to break.
Traffic flows again and all the town
seems right except for a few
corpuscles that stain the street
under a moth-beaten lamp light.

The Return

I saw myself in Miami today.
I need a broad. Wisconsin winters
and silent pockets
freeze me up. The snow-light
daze of December numbs my mind.
I don't have boots and live with mother.
It's colder than the shoulders
girls give me at the bar.

Jersey? Jersey is a bit of Wisconsin.
I'm alone. Pipes don't work;
I do, enough for groceries, rent.
I don't have a car, there are no buses,
cabs eat up my money—I eat pot pies.

I have no roots here. Miami in winter
is where I belong   neighbors calling
from windows   girls in bikinis   people
watering their lawns   pool parties   so many
days playing guitar on the sand.

Separated

Remember those rainbow, rubber ovals
puffed with magical gas,
how they stuck like lollipops to the roof
of our Buick, busted us
into fright with a pinch, when you weren't
watching, jumped away
in a breeze, diminishing into cinder
specks; the kite that lost
you in a sea-wind one March
off Island Beach. So I have
held that string of you
letting it slip from memory.

Historical Point

Each morning I pass it, catching
only, Huddy...March Twenty-eighth
1782...sometimes seeing... hanged.
The block house was burned; signs
of revolution smoked the air. Now
just another sign on Rt. 9—raised black
print on white background, wrought iron
curled and speared into the roadside.
It happened. And some days,
after I bridge the river, I find
myself riding into the morning sun
the noose of things I have done
heavy on my neck—a hero
of some sort. The houses behind me
burn; the revolution is in full fling.
All the Loyalists flee.

Each morning I pass it. The town
tore the old Stagecoach Tavern
down, dammed the river & left behind
this sign to remind me.

In Transit

The house tears loose from its
foundation—harbor of basement,
ties of pipes—sails, clipping
wind down river, forsythia
flying down black avenues,
into the bay, out to sea—
books shaking on their shelves,
windows, locks, glasses rattling.
Nails creak in their wooden beds,
wake to sun, salt. The white yacht
club and houses diminish. Long
since we drifted from tree lines
and sporty sailboats where men
with alligator emblems pointed at
us shouting. The shipping lanes
fail to cross us. Surviving the city,
we did not realize the limitless rim of ocean.
Another life under us, we don't open
cellar doors. I go for one more beer.
Making the best of the situation, you
turn on TV. There is no news of us.
Mary and John are whining for cartoons.
The sea begins to barnacle the doors
and, lately, TV reception has been poor.
You are growing bitchier, the children
whinier. Once, a jetliner—too high
to see us—with cocktails, dinners,
and laughing people whistled
by to shine somewhere on schedule.
We've gone too far. I miss the birds
but am lifted by porpoises who frolic
around the house. Whales spout
their fountains of hellos. Salt cakes
the chimney. We've given up
meat and potatoes. The kids tear into
sea turtle, and, once, a swordfish
leaped through our screendoor.
Lately, we've been receiving
B.B.C. programs. Oil slicks
have begun circling our house.

La Mare

You sea-smashing, rock-crashing roarer
Spraying spume, forging sky with fog,
Ghosty gulls, gongs of buoys—
Shroud in rags of seaweed, rich in decay
And tides—not even time can begin to tell
How they began—rise with plangent gods.
Out of your wave wakes the Lord of the Horses,
Gargoyled with the snakes of the sea, the gulls ghosting
Above him, blessing the trinity of his trident
And Proteus, that shepherd of the waves, there with the seal's
Shine, on rock, now rock itself, now wave
And Greece and Rome in the breakers—what prophecies!
You bitch of a sea, giving birth to the crab
And me, your beastial belly full of sextants,
Sailors and gods, release from Medusan swirls
Salt-white lightning—Pegasus in flight.

Sometimes I see what men have thought they saw:
Ahab's White Whale and Crane's Bridge in a fog.

Your riptides tear, your death-dreaming depths
Call galleons of minds to ponder, rapt
In your cadence. Homer, long dead, and blind
As a white wave, roars in your wine-dark rhythms.
What ships of fools grew confused on your curls
Of salt? What species broke from your belly
To inhabit the mind? Rusted, forever at bay,
Warning of strange moorings, bold buoys
Haunt the lighthouse of my night with gongs
And ride   wild white mares. *Mare Nostrum,*
Pacific and precipitous—and Rome thought you theirs.
Your bottom dreams their forms; sailors suspended
In salt fall free as men in space,
Their bones gamboling on the breakers of foreign sands.
La Mare—what voyages vein your womb!
Birth in the breakers and death in the depths—
The Scylla and Charybdis that wreck us all
Wait in the wag of your bull-bearing waves.
And what Christopher dared to cross your heart
With slow ships   as Icarus crossed the Sun?—
And Coleridge, who never crossed a sea, drags
With Rimbaud the ribs of your albatross.
There are witcheries in your waves, dreams in your depths;
Calliope cries in your redundant rounds
And Jonah, that Pinocchio of the Bible, pondering
Within a whale—Noah, half crazed with rain,
Bangs his bark together—decides his destiny.
Mia Mare, in isolated fields of grass, I kick up
Your broken shells and from pole to pole
Become: salt, waves— sea again.

Theresa Troise Heidel   "Summer Afternoon By The Auditorium"
9" x 11"   Watercolor   1996

Theresa Troise Heidel

"Ocean Grove Auditorium"
14" x 12"   Watercolor   1994
Private Collection

"Summer Light By The Tents"
8" x 12"   Watercolor   1992
Private Collection

The Pond

Before we came, she told us how they dug
a bowl of earth about fifteen meters
in diameter, lined it with heavy plastic
and put in a channel eight meters deep.
Those years, she would seek out swamps, inlets,
other waters for life she needed:
arrow arrum, water lilies, blue flag.
She stocked it with goldfish and tadpoles.
In summer, huge-eyed darning needles would stitch
patterns above the reeds. Water striders,
quick as the spots before your eyes, skated
its filmy surface. Once her husband built
a bridge, curved, with closely spaced slats—
an Oriental eyelid. Spiders would weave
their webs between lid and lashes of reeds.
At night, the eye of the pond would reflect moon
and trees. Through July and August, frogs quonking
in the barrel of night would wake her.

The first winter we lived there,
after the divorce, the river hardened,
cars went tobogganing, Florida
had snow in its palms. The goldfish
froze. A white iron set the contours
of the garden brittling leaves and limbs.
She remarried, sent her daughter to college.

Less wide-eyed with water, its reflection
broken by too many weeds, the eye could barely
see lilies wilting, turtles giving way
to toads. It sprang a leak the summer
water was precious. Hidden by reeds
in the garden's corner, it waited. She called
telling how hard it was to find a job.
She would go back to work in another field.

Five summers passed before we freed the pond,
pulling weeds, filling it with water, restocking:
arrow arrum, water lilies, blue flag.
In another field, she found love and work.
We repaired the bridge. Standing, one night,
we caught our reflection with moon and stars.

Late July. A leopard lily purring
orange-red, all its spots showing, sprang up.
The frogs quonked deep into the night.

The Violets

These violets reflect the violent
sea for their froth and bursting blue. Official
state flower of New Jersey they grow
in hobo jungles where they pour their waves
over soured-on life—and yesterday's
wine—tramps who like the weeds grew natural.

Violets catch my wife's nose and memory
by surprise. Vines of roots and rootlessness
hold her here, where as a girl she adventured—
stunned in honeysuckle and violets—
once, puzzling the bums with her beauty
till their leers drove her past those firefly lots.

Spring housing projects boom the lot and startle
the sky with steel—the tramps gone like fireflies
after a blink in twilight. She remembers
herself in cool blue smells of violets
and how all bloomed. The days descend. The tramps
grow romantic in her purple thoughts.

The Old Cat

The old cat won't stay buried.
She keeps riding the rain that drums the roof,
or stalks the moon until dawn.
Her tongue is in the rough wind licking the trees
clean. She is dragging her bobby sock under the bed
and clawing at the grey, empty toes.

She knows, I left her under
roots of pine, nine lives stiff as cones, only fur,
and light as birds, bones. Her eyes,
now, full of bright beetles, skull vacant and dark
as an abandoned beehive, her tail flicks at the roots.
She cannot take to the earth's ancient
embrace and purrs in the thunder
that threatens to uncover
her face.

The old cat is dragging out the sock again,
bringing in dreams that won't stay buried.

The Claws

Scattering of crab claws, sharp as stars, shadow
the sand. Castoffs, they lie hollow, mix
with driftwood, reeds, rope, cork, clamshells.
Like water-worn mussels that strewn the tide
line, they shine. Gulls pick them clean;
salt tides polish them. An ancient armor,
they gauntlet the beach now with empty threats.

Against the perpetual stride of the sea, sand
shifts ticking   ticking in the reeds   ticking
in the shells   ticking in the claws of the crabs—
above it all, a gull, mocking, mews.

Sun Prayer

Sun, destroyer of dew, let me
fly into your mouth—that hornet
of flames—be expelled through space
to warm whatever face
and rise again.

Sun, draw me up with the million molecules
of water that spark the grass
blades. Metamorphose me like insects
that pass in a rush of Falls from your rays.

Sun, with your shine of resurrections,
rise in my blood, undo
the cells of my brain. You, who
warms the worm in the rose
and multiplies the fish in the circle
of the zodiac, illuminate me
with your sacrament of flames.

Lion me, sun, with the rays of your mane.

Storm

All night the roarer from the sea
troubles our dreams, Morning: announcements
of powerless lines, school closings—
plunderings of the Atlantic. Outside
the whistler from the east drives whirls
of leaves down streets
spitting rain at them, garbage
takes on a life of its own, rebels
against its place. Boxes
use clumsy wings, fly
to perch on branches where they flap
hopelessly. Milked-out cartons
fill with white wind and go
tumbling off tops of curbs.
The saplings resist—their branches
cracking like eggshells. Last week's News
sputters at our panes and blasts
of wind make the television
a maniac of scribbles. Tomorrow
we will pick up
our lives and pile them
into green, plastic bags.
Morning. Wind lifts earth's
skirt, roars in our sleeves.

Night

The cat ears of moon move slowly
across my sky. Under my dark
habit, lover and murderer find sanctuary.
Unseen, I inhabit the mind, deep
below the brain coral of lost thoughts.
Unseen, in the meadow's black mass,
crickets attend my voice. Some hear me
in fissures that dendroid the earth, others
in the long-jawed skullholes of doors,
or in the orbits that oval the eyes.
I bring the dreams that sail you down to sleep.
I am wine—the sun's blood turned
black. In my womb everything waits
to grow—the owls are my eyes.

My Son Searching For Insects

looking for the mantis in its serrated prayer, parts Queen Anne's
lace and earth's grass skirt   to discover
fistfuls of green pebbles thrown hopping before him. Ricy stars
riddle the twilight. He stumbles
trying to grasp a wink in the weeds. Fireflies torn from their sexual
patterns light his unlabeled jar
with a cold glow   fill his sleep.   Sow the stars, son; summer's blood runs
in the grapevines. Woods are holy
with bugs. Watch carefully the black
widow's hourglass shape and who
collects who   in the jaws and webs   of time.

Spiders

While walking the bowling alley
parking lot, I find a spider
building its web in the open
window of my Ford. Sensing dead
beetles, flies, moths in the window's
web, I pluck the spider from its work,
and with a twig, whisk it onto
a nearby shrub. Now, every night
I walk there, I glance, checking
for a rebuilt web, All I find
is one, long dragline hanging from
the top of the bush to the ground.

Lifting picnic benches
so the landlord can paint,
the underside of one
startles us. A dense web
with Q-tip egg sacs sticks
to a dark joint. Stranded
in web are husks of spiders,
Japanese beetles &
disembodied
wings of moths like lost
kites. Erupting from one
sac, hundreds of wiggling
spiders fan out to build
their own worlds where
they hang & wait.

Late August. Spiders string
their webs from pine trees to poles.
Between wires, orbs of webs
fix their eyes into the wind.
A thousand spiders hang heavy in the air.
Their eyes beacon the insect dark.

Three million centuries of instinct.

Crow

CAW   CAW   woke me   scratching
through a menagerie of   dreams
all   i could recall was
scorched cry   flap of wings
rising over river mists   leaving
claw prints of   pine

The Geese

   They arrived around Labor Day. I was never sure what kind of geese they
were—the male was white, the female gray—but they never went farther
south than the Toms River. I always saw them together, usually on the lawns
of the houses across the street, one watching the other feed a few feet away.
They mated for life. Coming home along Riverside Drive after a rough day
at work, I would slow to see if they were still there. It somehow calmed me
to know they were. On bright mornings, it cheered my spirits to see the white
goose on a deep-green lawn.
   Some time in early May, a seventeen-year-old boy ran over the male.
Witnesses said the car had been speeding around a blind bend and could not
stop in time. Now there are two duck-crossing signs along Riverside, but they
are too late. The gray goose, after several weeks of mournful honking, moved
up the river to Windy Cove.

skid marks merge
with twilight shadows...
the call of the goose
unanswered

Prose by Frank Finale
Haiku by Rich Youmans

Gulls

Carving a salt sky, they drift on swells of air, bellies matching
the feathered caps that wave below them. Inland, they sweep over
grapnel sea-smells of dumps. Navying
the white tide for food, they find stars.

I saw one on Ocean Avenue   early   rising
with a clam shell, releasing and descending
to pick it clean. Deeper into that avenue,
I saw some smashed thing, the ends of its wings fluttering
in the breeze. Driving home, the tail of my eye
caught hundreds swaying as in some ritual,
wind in their feathers, pencil-pilings of their legs
anchored to the tide line, eyes barnacled to the sea.

Tonight, I dream the dream of flying again.
Floating in the shell of a mussel-blue sky, I see
myself driving on Ocean Avenue. Alarmed, I awake
and try to dream the dream of the gulls again.

Horseshoe Crabs

I fear the crabs, feel their pincers plying my skin,
picking at the mind's flaws.
See that humped horseshoe with tapered spike that seems to float
above the grains and flounce
like a pugilist when poked. Upset it. Stare at the underside

of fright. Legs, jointed like spiders, writhe for webs
of seaweed, rocks and water,
scramble like insects brought to light from underworlds
of damp stones—claws waging
a war with air, a spike carefully wheedling

the wind. Paleozoic crawlers, their armor-
awkward species survived
the dinosaur and war, their shapes lie beached
and form a trail of lost
horseshoes for mud, sand and time to record.

In the shell of night, in the mythy mind, the crabs rule.
Spiny, adept with claws,
they crawl, black-brown, from a dragon-hissing sea of sleep
up to feast on
some forgotten fear; some shape too distant to remember.

Unlearning

I am unlearning books I read   words
I knew
I am unlearning numbers and   the religion
I learned   by heart
sun and moon   begin
to educate me
trees are an alphabet   stars
a higher one
the flight of the geese teaches   even stones
speak   are spirited
I am unlearning mother   father
the relatives
and beginning to see   energy
that vibrates
around us   lives within all   last night
i heard   rain
today i read the intricacies of   a leaf

        and forgot

        my own name

The House

For all those years they swatted flies,
vacuumed dust, kept plates clean, settled
down to TV, somewhere flies
were buzzing, dust tumbleweeding
out of the corners, plates multiplying
beyond legend. But there, they kept
the fort against natural things, till
they grew too old—the things
too many. Webs in corners vibrated
with spiders and beetles; old journals
grew ceiling-high, yellowing
the library; dust took the chatter
from the plates. Vines entered
the veins of their windows, mingled
with the splintered beams. A rose—all thorns—
grew in the guest's bed, and cracked shoes
housed a colony of roaches;
the rain seemed a welcome guest.
In the weeds a FOR SALE sign grew.

Sunday

Through the east windows, sun
slants a little higher this month.
The cats have just been fed.
Each finds its patchwork
sunlight to preen
under. From the frying pan, eggs
and bacon begin
their morning chatter
leaking the flavors
of their conversation
into the air. Still
in pajamas, I skim
the news. Under the sheet, one
foot out, my wife
is drawn from her dreams by
scents of coffee and bacon. Mourning
doves flock about the feeder.
Above them, leaves
vibrate with light. A reflection
off the silverware catches
the cats' eyes; simply
buttering bread, I break
into joy.

Theresa Troise Heidel   "Tents In Early Evening Light"
9" x 12"   Watercolor   1995   Private Collection

All Hallow's Eve

Scorpio waits in horoscape for demons,
goblins. Fill the bags before Jack snaps
summer's apples into winter and all
the leaves witch it from bones of trees.
Scarecrows, werewolves. Quick. The dead
do not forget us. This night smells
of candle wax and smoke. There is more
than winter chill in the air. Listen
to the wind in the elms. A thin melody skeletons
the shadows. Light the bonfire to remind
us of sun. Watch carefully the cold,
stone shoulders of the graveyard. Someone
wants to dance. Scorpio hooks
its starry tail into the hallowed dark.

The Pumpkin

October. Finished gouging. The pumpkin
holds a candle to
our window. Like a moon,
it fills the sill
and glowers in the dark.

The upward arrows of its eyes flicker.
Its mouth, drawn down
by flame and gravity, casts a sickle
on the porch screen.
Heat lopsides the sharp nose.

Some stray seeds remain in the singed gourd
and heat brings out
a damp sweet smell from the hollowed insides—
vegetable spit
oozes with candle's wax.

Morning—leaves are ripe, turn in suns like fire—
opals, shifting
in fields of light. This afternoon, born—
out of clear sky
wisp of sickle—daylight moon.

The Tormentors

I have seen them at night
mad as mares,
wearing their souls on their sleeves
and fiddling at their hearts.

I have heard their veins running
through the leaves,
scraping darkly at the oaks,
scratching strange names on the boughs.

I have smelled their shared hair
on the cold
Canadian winds, stiff as pines,
cutting as cones.

I have know them womb deep,
thick in the blood
through rubs of dark and wisps of shapes,
and always, they disperse by light.

The Age Of Faith

At night these houses are lighted ships,
sails of curtains flying from second story
windows as they hold their cargo
of families under steep hands-of-prayer
roofs, silently above a highway
of lamplights and below a ream of stars.
So many possibilities bud and leaf
under the wooden roofs and beanstalk moon:
a Jack grows up to be a giant-killer;
a Jill becomes a surgeon; Hansel
and Gretel turn jewelers. On the highway
below them, headlights follow
three glowing trails into the night.

In The Attic

Here, in the attic, floorboards warp
from leaks that rain; the chimney
(now extinct) is cracked—mortar
between bricks flakes off. Here,
close to beams, weary
with sun, bird life and winds
plague the timber with ghosts. Inside,
radiators hunt up a heat to keep
weather away, nails in beams show through, grow
thin with rust. The carpenters all
dead, like Christ, their energy spent, their work
stands still—rots, takes root.
Without insulation, I see patterns
of crossbeams, hear forest hauntings,
feel the sacrifice of pine
to an architecture of forgotten times.

Horror Story

There is always a man with suns in his torch.
He leads the calm ones off their summer porches,
Out of tavern sounds and the reek of ale.
Out to kill, he shouts the standard rail
And holds a noose made from someone's hair;
Guillotines shine in his eyes, "You men, follow the rear!"

i am in a castle   always   electricity

zapping from tendrils

of wires   chemicals gargling

from test tubes   when they knock with

a dead tree   i answer

in another tongue   my scars   still dark

Luck

Rabbits & clover, rainbows & pennies,
devils & stones—take them
all; they hardly ever bring the lucre
of luck. It is the bison-backed
ocean that buffaloes the sight,
web-dewed pines that catch the mind in flight.
The wind augers the weather;
the seasons fly like pepper.
Beside me these remain: pencil, books,
some wine, guitar (in background), a little
light and a cat in the shadows.

Mass Of Flames

Morning—Christ's cross in ghosts of smoke,
Bells sounded bitter and flames licked
The cellar bright, drove it beyond its height,
Fired up three stories—two burning suns,
One fastened infernally to space,
One here, outside my crossed window.
In the monolithic church
Where bells rang clear as sea once,
Water gushed through reels of hoses,
Fell on the candle lit by God
And froze my eyes in morning cold.
Fire and water-sacraments—
Elements of a different nature,
Turned to tear down a house of God.
By His stones an eighty-eight year old priest stood,
Threatened to burn with the beams,
Till whiskey-warm firemen persuaded him away.
    It is late, night blends with trees' shapes
    Shades of fire, smells of smoke,
    November, and only the fire-blisters
    That drumlin the door gleam sadistically
    Their thousand smiles.

Necromancers

Caught up in their theories, their eyes dilate.
They leave the institution   striking out
on their own   who will fund them?
Finding building and machinery, they need
brain and body to complete the experiment.
They impress their guests by serving white wine
with trout, astound their colleagues by hinting
how close to breaking through they are.

After twelve, in the basement behind bolted
doors, shadows stalk the test tubes. One
wears a mask, holds a gleam in his hand.
The other assists. There's electricity
in the air. Winding down   the staircase flickers
with the insomnia of a nightgowned girl.
The hunchback hauls his sack into
the bat-flapping dark. Over the swamp   a mist
white as a surgeon's gown   rises.
In the end, all their experiments light
the dark woods   in an accident of flames
                    the secrets are lost.

Margaret Tourison Berndt   "Quack Attack"
36" x 48"   Acrylic   1995   Collection of Van Kampen Group   Prints Available

Windows, Toys, & Ice

Rice-white gardens, grasses
of glass in streams of sunlight click—
the noonday star rises, catches
its height, captures the eyes
in the ice. With a cold weight, wires
sag/break creating violets
in the dangerous air. Avenues
run rivers of ice
under sworded boughs. Parabolas
of frost span whole displays of
G.I. Joes & model trains. Today
I find the needles
in the snowstacks   shining   my eyes
        nuclear with joy.

Walking On Ice

Two boys quiz the frozen bay with light steps.
Farther out, iceboats triangle the horizon.
Thirty-two degrees, but surely safe. The boys' shadows
string along, obliquely, crablike on ice.
One, his left leg sliding back too far, right
moving forward too slowly, follows.
I remember my fourteen-year-old son
following a shadow on ice when it cracked
and sent him shooting down; the younger one,
waiting, caught him on the pop up.
Air pockets and luck delivered him from the ice
hole—a rebirth of sorts. Crying, they hugged
each other till their shivery arrival at our steps
where mom asked, "And where have you been!"

The Snowman

Gleaming in moonshine, a snowman stares,
his corncob pipe fixed into the pebbles
of a frozen smile. Time has made hard
his vegetable eyes. Silhouetted
he wears a magician's hat, holds
a witch's broom, watches the house
where the luminous face of the girl
who shaped him peers through the frost
feathered pane of her bedroom window.
One rise of mercury, he can change.
But tonight   a cold night   in full moon
he stands wed to the   white   earth

The Firs

I saw the firs, uprooted, spidery from earth,
their roots still dark with a life
brought to surface, and how silent with secrets,
stoic to seasons and evergreen
beyond the push of death. Under the moon's
counterfeit light, I envisioned man
in machines bulldoze the life out of earth.
I saw him spawn his stores
that did not breathe and had no roots.
When night, I'd cup my ear
to floor, hear the growth that stretched the dark
and feel the crack of concrete.

At Christmas, firs come to haunt us.

From The Corner

this pine, ten-thousand
sharps high, evergreen
to its point, needles the air
electric—elves, reindeer,
tinsel forever
falling between branches
all under the ceiling
star. You stare at light—
forest of Bethlehem
blue, thorn-wound red,
North Pole white, a noel
of needles shadowing
floor. Breathing
the ginny nearness of
its trunk, the scent
of all your Christmases rushes
warm before you.

Before Bed

wind swirls
snow around
lamplight
stars like van Gogh.
Snow bandages
bare elms
black blooded
boulevards; a celebration
a non-existent
parade where
joy crystallizes
in a child's eyes
who praising
kneels at
the yellow lighted
dormer window.

Survival

When dinosaurs scaled the conifers, cold came;
cold wasted the elephants
of Hannibal's army, caught Napoleon's men,
cast Washington in Valley Forge,
chained the helmets of Hitler. The conifers are still
with us   and the cold.

Wings of snow crystal the window.
Pines, silent in their silhouettes, procession the sky.
Heir to the mountain and cold,
they prefix their drop of cones to the moss's secret
and the lichen's everlastingness.

Winter Complaint

A smell of snow in air, sounds grow distant, break-
down of clouds—a rush in the market
before winter's scent. Swarms of flakes
merry-go-round the air, begin
to simplify the streets. Late
that day, the sky went, avenues lost
their names, lines fell. A ghost on TV
keeps rising. I am stunned by silence
and the smile of ice that sleeps in my blood.

I heard of loves that howled for form,
and of western winds that brought down the rain,
and of longings for lovers during storms,
but this frolicking of snow
stings me cold, liquidates its shape
and leaves no honey in my bed.

Virginia Perle   "Sunset On The Toms River"
18" x 23"   Watercolor   1997
Collection of Ocean County Cultural & Heritage Commission   Prints Available

To My Mother

in a field of daisies   how easily
you photograph—flowery pinafore
and white teeth camouflaged among white
petals. Strands of your black hair lift
with wind, are lost in el-dark woods. You wear
a scarf, your brown eyes floating above this
sea of eyes. Soon you will meet the earth.
But, here, life rises to meet your senses.
I wonder who shuttered this glimpse
of you   we carry with us
a crushed rose in the Bible of ourselves?

Louie

My brother, in full moon, drunk on Bud and bourbon,
across from the station where he pumped
Gulf gas, wrestled pythons of hoses to the tank
and oil made rainbows
in September puddles—
stared at his boots, smeared with grease,
recalled gears' growls, hot breath of motors—
dreamed of love.

Leaving python, pump, columns of want ads strewn on
bed, grease stains on rugs (his Jersey
rainbows shaken), he craved city's cradle of stone,
triangles of white
collars, less strain, more sex.
August. Mementos, oil and salt air,
breathe back his Labor Day binge, that search
for a lost Ford.

Jimmy

One bright Sunday in June, walked out
from his boarded house, the spring in his
stiff shoes making his step faster, the jays
screaming as he passed over sidewalks'
weathered cracks (where earth's vegetable
energy grew back)—the lions of suns
roaring on the bay three blocks away
and pines sighing a hundred dark forms
against the salted sky—walked past
Miss Britton's splendid garden where the brine
grew on the dew and insect eggs
were hatching noisily, past the screeching
McGees who owned a junk yard full of gleams
(metals and children), across the avenues
that ran like black rivers—there were no stop signs,
past the terrible vacancy of lots
on to the loose whirls of quartz that filled
the displaced crabs, the broken reeds, the empty
containers—a blitz of beer cans and clam
shells clattering before the cattle of his shoes—
walked into the first wave before his
breakfast, while the town was still sleeping.

Plane Choice

The last thing your wife said to you was,
"Damn well not be late. One thing
I hate is waiting in some rinky-dink
airport for your flight to come in."

The last time you flew, your three-piece suit
was ringed with sweat, and you stayed
at the airport bar longer than needed,
trying to convince yourself
of safety records—planes versus cars.

You postpone your fear, decide to chauffeur
us to D.C., fly back to Jersey alone.
After driving the Mustang over bridges
that could tumble, tunnels that could swallow
you up and by trailers that could swoop you
out of your lane with one fast pass,
three days later, you pace
a living room in D.C. giggling
about disaster flights and gremlins
on the wing. Airport officials request
you show up forty-five minutes early.
That same day, we amble about
the National Air and Space Museum looking
at showcases, memorabilia & planes
hanging over everything like schedules.

It begins to drizzle. Saying our goodbyes,
you look for insurance. In rain, you board
the plane of your nightmares. No stewardess
can help you. You sit among empty seats.
The plane delayed, there are no drinks. You wait
an hour for a half-hour flight. While you   bump
over cobble-clouded sky into the New Jersey
night, someone in Atlantic City waits
rattled as dice over your late departure.

The Gathering

Little pieces of me keep falling
off, swirling in wind, drifting
in cycles of air & water.

I am piecing the selves
together—my lost names that
time winked away

in cellars where we showed
our hidden features at six & at universities
where we displayed our wits.

Down river meeting ourselves
our names have
changed. I am my grandfather.

Imperceptibly as
shadows of ants, bits of me keep
falling away—

drifting leaves against
a snowfence. Grandfather.
I mark where the river

turns into the bay.
I rock & hear
the creaking of dawn.

Emptying myself into
the light, I keep the river
of your voices in my blood.

Poe

Someone from The Baltimore Sun finds you
in a tavern. Four days later, a specter
of yourself, you die alone.
                                They named a street
in Jersey after you. Only the asphalt
has the look of your eyes. Most who live there
remember you as raving mad   or
for some horror story.
Another critical biography of you
appears. The cat scratches to be let out.
In the shadows of the Osprey Tavern
I glimpse Baudelaire's albatross.
An obsidian-eyed raven drags
his wings into the modern age.

In Baltimore, pigeons flock to your statue.

Making The Rounds

The wagon circles—eight Clydesdale horses
pull the prickly cases. Bottle-stiff
two men in captain's caps hold the reins
and six, silent-barking dogs follow.
These are the wheels I come back to after
making the rounds. Earth too, circling, increasing
its weight—ten-thousand pounds of meteoric
dust each year—rounder now—not the same
Earth   or people   horses   or dogs. Yet, wheels keep
turning in cogs of clocks and gears of cars.
It is the wheel of the solar system now,
turning within the galaxy—itself
turning in the dark. On Earth: great
water cycles, day & night, planting & reaping.
But on great and small wheels
all things change—only the wheeling remains
turning about atoms, stars. . . I came
to see the BUDWEISER wagon again, silently
carouseling its shadows above bartender, patron,
waitress and the spirits that wheel within us and
about us, circling all things we see. And do not.

Stranger Passing

The man moves with half-steps and taps of wood.
The window frames his figure only a moment.
My eyes settle on his scarecrow form, mind
strains to think me in his bones—his gray coat
forecasting early winter. Languid
as the moon entangled in branches
of maple, he moves, and where maple hides
the view, eyes presume to see the snail feet.
Once past pole and webs of leaves, place where
I expect him to appear, there is only
space and a few fallen leaves that hug the wind.

Losing God

When a child, bound by parents to stay near the house,
the horizon to me was God. Neither earth   nor sky
it existed   like the light from extinguished stars.
Always there   at the perimeter of my vision   something
I could never place a finger on. And beyond   the farthest
I could see   *more God*, the edge, the rim. I stood
in the middle of the street and peered   down the elm-leafy
tunnel   like the wrong end of a telescope   till I grew
dizzy   God small   but never ending. At Coney Island
I could see Him   at his most expansive   in the horizon
just beyond the egret   of a slim sail.
Grasping the thick twist of rope   at the farthest barrel
I would bound up   from the baptism of a wave
salt burning my eyes   and behold   Him in the horizon
     there   but always exceeding my reach   like the image
that keeps repeating   in double mirrors   smaller
and smaller   till nothing   is left

A Love Poem?

My wife begs me to write a love poem.
    "About whom?"
    "Me, of course. You wrote me one before you met me."
    "Yeah, but that was layered with phrases like 'a diamond in the rough,' 'a flower ready to blossom.'"
    "Well, I *was* back then!"
    "But love poems are so hard to write. It's all been said before."
    "Yes, but I'm tired of everyone asking me, 'Has he ever written you a love poem?'"
    "Just tell them, 'No, he's too close to me to be able to write about me closely.'"
    "But you write about everyone else: your mother, your father, your brother, our children."
    "That's different!"
    "How is it different? You don't love them?"
    "No, I mean, *yes*, but I'm *away* from them."
    "You've been with me over twenty years and, admit it, you can't write a love poem about me."
    "Not without mentioning how wonderful you are or how beautifully I see you."
    "What's wrong with that?"
    "Two centuries of love poems that said it before and better."
    "Then write a negative love poem—*something*."
    "That's been done too. 'My clumsiest dear, whose hands shipwreck vases....'
How about that one I started, 'In the columns of her dailiness—*McCall's, Family Circle*....'"
    "You never finished it. Besides, I'm not that woman anymore."
    "You're right. That's *one* of the reasons I love you."
    "Oh? What are the others?"
    "I've told you them before."
    "Tell me again."
    "There goes another love poem."

Garage Organist

While the Volkswagen weathers the seasons,
the church organ is parked inside.
He calls it his great whore and is not afraid
to spend his time and money on her.
Each time I visit, a change: pipes
stored in attic, others taken
down again (more range), wires re-vein
the floor, jigsaws of wood lie
with sawdust over fading grease spots.
For the third time this year, he breaks her
down, rebuilds, extends the garage, plays
fugues from Bach that ring in her pipes.
Once, long after his fingers stopped,
he swore he could hear her breathe, pumped
up, waiting to play cathedrals.

Dick LaBonté   "Temperature 62°"

18" x 24"   Acrylic   1978   Collection of Mr. and Mrs. Albert H. Davis III   Prints Available

Dick LaBonté
"The Bluffs Bar"
12" x 20"   Acrylic   1984
Collection of Artist   Prints Available

Last Day

Squinting into heat, we pose:
front row kneeling on green tarp over
brown grass, next row settling on chairs,
then the retirees and others leaving
for greener pastures; a last tier of teachers
standing on benches, this new height altering
their view of the school ground. After each shutter
of the camera, McGruff, the stuffed dog, is passed
to another retiree, so one proof can be
distinguished from another. The kneelers
hold the banner—place & year. They feel
as though they're back in church atoning
for their sins. The photographer, in the picture
too, leaves his place, hustles to check
the camera's distant eye.
Dashing back to his space, he huffs, "Last one.
Pass McGruff!"
                        Then it's over.
Eighty teachers, administrators and
secretaries rise on their cramped legs or step
down from their benches and away from
the neat frame of the photo to disperse
into the wavy air of summer.

Summer Recess

Bengal-yellow buses roar the children
away. Like lightning bugs before dark,
here and there, janitors appear in doorways.
Late shift: empty lavatory stalls,
offices, classrooms.
The knock of a broom echoes in a stairwell.

Too long steeped in teaching children,
I reflect on sun motes,
the terrible silence of corridors;
hear click of time and teachers, passed and
passing. Wind whispers through cracks.

The last grade is penned into the record book.
Outside, geraniums hold the summer
light and send their seeds flying.

Long Division

The nine o'clock bells are ringing. It is past bedtime—mine.
Father keeps smacking his palm on his forehead, trying
to make me understand. It begins to snow: all numbers
mix, place value loses its place, remainders startle.
Again, father smacks his forehead. I creak upstairs, sleep,
     forget;   I dream   white
     crystal   geometries

Looking For Miss Gordon

I walk through corridors abandoned
by students and low slants of sun.
Somewhere an electric hum keeps the building
warm as breath. Flinging open
a door to a lost room, I hear
the silence of name tags. Desks lie
empty as a skull's stare.
Outside, wind plays, whistling in
the monkey bars, and rings of chopped pines
record a broken marriage
to the weather. The parking lot is pebbles.

Kay Wheeler

teacher, principal, forty-three years without
an absence, your record, older than half
the teachers teaching, stands. When you retired,
they gave you a certificate. Schools choose
springy Arbor Days to plant trees to honor
students taken by rare brain diseases, teachers
snipped away by accidents, war heroes
who gave their limbs. In April days,
after school, waiting for my ride home, I read
the bronze plaques and wonder at their raised names.
And now   what will they do with you
who broke the male, female barrier
running a school, showing up every day
for forty-three years? Another April.
A thousand seeds are dispersed among
orchards of your students and teachers,
and there, they send down roots. There,
your tree flowers their thoughts.

Kenny

State champ and national record holder
at seventeen, married at eighteen,
refusing scholarships because his wife
could not live in with him. Divorced now
and remarried, he downs his Schaefer,
tells me how he could have gone to college.
The bartender towels the bottle zeros
from the bar and rings up another round.

Elementary

The gifted girl who wrote a letter
to the custodian on why the apple tree should
not be cut down. It wasn't.

The arthritic boy—absent on damp days—
whose brother carried his books home
from school, every day.

The girl who loved snakes, raised them,
dreamed, drew & wrote
stories about them.

The cheerleader who rarely took off
her cheerleading jacket, could barely
do math but won the music talent show.

The energetic child with perfect attendance
who was always there to collect
papers, wash the board, answer questions.

The boy who scowled at directions, shunned
those who tried to help him, yet
loved Garfield the cat.

The older girl who could not read
& whose grandfather abused her &
her mother before her.

The boy who found his hanged father
in the garage & gazed—beyond
daily lessons—at crows in the field.

More varied than combinations of letters
of the alphabet which border
the chalkboard & line the room,
another class files in. Quietly waits.

Virginia Perle   "Summer Fun"
14" x 18"   Watercolor   1996   Private Collection   Prints Available

Julio

lies basking on sewer pipe (his hard
hat reflecting points of sun), chats
about roller derby, his
guitar, Puerto Rico, wrestling,
welfare. His pregnant wife in
the hospital, his six children wait
for supper—rice and beans. He grows
salty for his salary. Spading
machine-bitten dirt back around
the pipe, he tells how he escaped
by pole vaulting the fence of the migrant
workers' camp that brought him here.
There is something about him—not
the shine of sweat or friend-like hand
he extends when you want to jump
out of a ditch dense with the odor
of rotting roots. Dreaming, playing
numbers while power-hoe and crew
idle, he waits for the next
pipe—hums an island tune.

Laborer

Jesus: fat, forty, married
to a sixteen-year old black, working
for a baby that keeps him awake
all night, a television he's too tired
to watch, still down in the mud rinsing
his hands in a puddle, mumbles in Spanish.

After lunch—a few beers—like lizards,
we loll in the sun. They speak
of Puerto Rico, memories of easiness,
dream of going back—we quit soon.

Already, the power-hoe begins to idle
waking us from dreams of green islands,
numbing our ears as it digs our ditch
dark and rich with the stench of roots.

Construction Worker

Driving to work on Rt. 37 West
he spots two white-tail deer bloating
on the side of the road. He carries them
in his thoughts to the work site. There he leaves
his Chevy, slaps on his yellow hard hat
and begins to shamble down the stripped slope.
The rest of the crew is already drinking
Seven-Eleven coffee. Before he reaches them
an old woman searching for her house wanders
up to him. She has been away
two weeks in Florida and did not realize
another section had been added to
the village, another piece that looks the same
as the one before it, five variations
of houses repeating their pattern;
at the main entrance, a new funeral parlor.

In the unfinished sector, a whirlwind
begins lifting leaves and dust. Out-dated newspapers
pulled into circulation
swirling from foundation to foundation, suddenly
lose energy,
drop. Workers in T-shirts snap
metal bands from a pallet of pipe.
Working in sync, they string out a few hours' worth of work.
Blindingly bright, pipes reflect in sun,
forecast a hot day. The backhoe clanks
into place, begins its methodical pawing
at the earth. Like the hours ahead of them, the trench lengthens,
He, too, becomes lost in the labyrinth,
the deer having slipped his mind which now tracks
the sun's arc to the end of the day. Quitting time,
the trench filled, the pipe connected, a ghost
of dust follows each worker's car out;
at home, it reappears in their handkerchiefs.

That night he dreams of the old woman floating
away from the village; two white-tail deer
follow: past the funeral parlor, above
the yellow machines and whizzing cars
on Rt. 37, toward the horizon till they fade,
three commas in an invisible sentence.

The Exterminator

My spray tank full, pumped, I prepare,
descending cellar steps, to kill the roach,
whose antennae the tombs of Egypt knew,
the spider, who spun through the mansions
of Ur, the fly, whose myriad eye saw
the blood of Jesus go sweet on the cross.
Below, the scarab's husk cracks
under my heel and newspapers scuttle
with life. In the beams, termites
riddle my house with questions.

Sign Man

One summer, just off the beach,
you knocked at our door—wearing
black shoes and socks, hair slicked
back, bathing suit pulled tightly
to your crotch, pale skin—looking
as though you had just taken off
your Lone Ranger mask and stepped out
of a porn flick from the fifties.
You asked my wife if I could
work for a couple of hours.

In the cab of your hand-me-down cherry picker,
you rework the details of our next job
for which we are three weeks late.
When we arrive the owner bitches,
but your prices are cheap, her summer season
short. Accepting your cheesy smile, she points
to where she needs her signs.
Overdrawn at the bank   each summer
you watch your secretaries come
and go—too many complaints,

too little pay.
Stopping work, your workers help you
look for your keys. You find them
in your pocket. The business near
bankrupt, your plastic ship
plunges. Three years later
in a new store
with another name,
it resurfaces, and I spy you
still at the helm, waving.

Ritual

I dream of mythical monsters, loss of limbs
and loved ones, falling, but always the mail
is delivered. The dream on pause, I spot
the mail just coming or leaving. The last
delivery—Brooklyn—two white, self-addressed
envelopes. Taking the mail up to mother
(I have not even written yet), she opens
Bell bills, car payments, other junk. I open
envelopes with the familiar script—one,
an acceptance; another, a request (I am
fourteen years old)—some minor revisions.

It is Manasquan, Jersey—a boarding house
where I stay after college (I'm twenty-three).
On the porch, envelopes, packages overflow
spilling on to the wicker chair below. I open
the junk ones first, saving as mom did, best
for last. I tremble over my self-addressed
New Yorker, Atlantic envelopes—
to which I never sent anything!
The dream begins to dissolve.

In the first house I remember, grandma
upstairs, bedridden and dying, the mail
downstairs (I am five years old). The box clips
are a bowtie of white—magazines, bills,
four self-addressed envelopes. I am thirsty, go
for water. Before I return, I awake.

Mythical monsters, living,
falling, dying, yet the mail is delivered,
and always, I am there to receive.

Paula Kolojeski   "Fisherman's Cove Bait Shack"
17" x 24"   Pastel   1994   Private Collection   Prints Available

Paula Kolojeski
"Carlson's Corner"
17" x 24"   Pastel   1991
Private Collection   Prints Available

Appendix To The Stories And Essays

Books and publications in which the stories and essays in this book were originally published.

Anthologies:

A Loving Voice II: A Caregiver's Book Of More Read-Aloud Stories For The Elderly, Carolyn Banks and Janet Rizzo, editors, The Charles Press, Publishers, Inc., 1994

First Light: Poems, Stories And Essays Of The Winter Holiday Season, Susan Richardson, editor, Calypso Press, 1997

Identity Lessons, Contemporary Writing About Learning To Be American, Maria Mazziopti Gillan and Jennifer Gillan, editors, Penguin Books, 1999

Shore Stories, Rich Youmans, editor, Down The Shore Publishing, Harvey Cedars, NJ, 1998

Literary and College Journals and Magazines:

Footwork: The Paterson Literary Review, Passaic County Community College, Paterson, NJ, Issue 23, 1993

Raconteur, Susan Carroll Publishing, Williamsburg, VA, July 1995

Without Halos, The Ocean County Poets Collective, Point Pleasant Beach, NJ, Volume VIII, 1991

Magazines:

COAST Magazine, The Valente Publishing House, Inc., Bay Head, NJ, various editions 1986 – 1991,

COAST Magazine's Jersey Shore Almanac, The Valente Publishing House, Inc., Bay Head, NJ, 1990 and 1991 editions

Down Memory Lane, Dobbs Publishing Group, Inc., Lakeland, FL, December/January 1993

New Jersey Outdoors, New Jersey Department Of Environmental Protection, Trenton, NJ, Winter 1998

Reminisce EXTRA, Reiman Publications, Greendale, WI, December 1994 (appeared titled as "His Holidays Were Lionel Days")

The 1990 Guide Book Of The Greater Point Pleasant Area Chamber Of Commerce, The Valente Publishing House, Inc., Bay Head, NJ, 1990

Newspapers:

The Asbury Park Press, September 25, 1993

The Beachcomber, The Sandpaper, Inc., Surf City, NJ, August 15, 1998; July 4, 1998; July 18, 1998

The Christian Science Monitor, Des Moines, IA, 1991

Appendix To The Poems

Books and publications in which the poems in this book were originally published.

THE JERSEY SHORE:

"Twilight Lake" first appeared in **Under A Gull's Wing**, edited by Frank Finale and Rich Youmans, Down The Shore Publishing, Harvey Cedars, NJ, 1996

"Sea Oats: Island Beach State Park" first appeared in **COAST Magazine** (November 1988), The Valente Publishing House, Inc., Bay Head, NJ

"Seascape: Manasquan, NJ" first appeared in **POEM** (#16, 1972), The Huntsville Literary Association, Huntsville, AL; **COAST Magazine** (August 1987), The Valente Publishing House, Inc., Bay Head, NJ; **Under A Gull's Wing**, edited by Frank Finale and Rich Youmans, Down The Shore Publishing, Harvey Cedars, NJ, 1996

"Reign Of Fire: Asbury Park" first appeared in **Plains Poetry Journal** (1983), Jane Greer, editor, Bismarck, ND

"River Watch" first appeared in **Under A Gull's Wing**, edited by Frank Finale and Rich Youmans, Down The Shore Publishing, Harvey Cedars, NJ, 1996

"Point Pleasant Beach" first appeared in **Black Buzzard Review** (1997), Bradley R. Strahan, editor, Arlington, VA; **Ocean County Library** (bookmark), April 1998

"Last Stop" first appeared in **Press Quarterly** (1997), Daniel Roberts, Inc., New York, NY; **Shore Stories**, edited by Rich Youmans, Down The Shore Publishing, Harvey Cedars, NJ, 1998

"Laird's Applejack (Monmouth, N. J., 1698)" first appeared in **Exit 13** (1995), Tom Plante, Fanwood, NJ

"Jersey Shore Vacation Again" first appeared in **Vacation Week** (1986), George Valente, editor and publisher

"The Fishermen: Island Beach State Park" first appeared in **COAST Magazine** (November 1985), The Valente Publishing House, Inc., Bay Head, NJ; **Under A Gull's Wing**, edited by Frank Finale and Rich Youmans, Down The Shore Publishing, Harvey Cedars, NJ, 1996

"Island Beach State Park" first appeared in **Under A Gull's Wing**, edited by Frank Finale and Rich Youmans, Down The Shore Publishing, Harvey Cedars, NJ, 1996

"Fishermen" first appeared in **the new renaissance** (vol. X, #2, 1998), Louise T. Reynolds, editor, Arlington, MA

"City Girl At Seaside Heights" first appeared in **Journal Of New Jersey Poets** (vol. IV, #1, 1979), County College Of Morris, Randolph, NJ; **COAST Magazine** (August 1984), The Valente Publishing

House, Inc., Bay Head, NJ; **Under A Gull's Wing**, edited by Frank Finale and Rich Youmans, Down The Shore Publishing, Harvey Cedars, NJ, 1996

"On The Boardwalk At Point Pleasant Beach" first appeared in **Under A Gull's Wing**, edited by Frank Finale and Rich Youmans, Down The Shore Publishing, Harvey Cedars, NJ, 1996

"The Galleon" first appeared in **New Collage** (1973-74), A. McA. Miller, Sarasota, FL; **COAST Magazine** (Holiday 1991), The Valente Publishing House, Inc., Bay Head, NJ

"Tail End, Summer" first appeared in **DeKalb Literary Arts Journal** (Winter 1988), DeKalb College, Clarkston, GA

"The Return" first appeared in **The Brooklyn Review** (#5, 1988), Brooklyn College, Brooklyn, NY

"Separated" first appeared in **Journal Of New Jersey Poets** (1976), County College Of Morris, Randolph, NJ; **COAST Magazine** (May 1984), The Valente Publishing House, Inc., Bay Head, NJ

"Historical Point" first appeared in The Asbury Park Press

"In Transit" first appeared in **Gryphon** (1983), The College Of Arts and Letters At The University Of South Florida, Tampa, FL; **COAST Magazine** (Autumn 1991), The Valente Publishing House, Inc., Bay Head, NJ

"La Mare" first appeared in **North American Mentor Magazine** (1977), John Westburg Associates, Fennimore WI

NATURE:

"The Pond" first appeared in **Princeton Spectrum** (1983); **New Jersey Poetry Journal** (1985), West Long Branch, NJ

"The Violets" first appeared in **Snowy Egret** (1969), Humphrey A. Olsen, Bowling Green, IN

"The Old Cat" first appeared in **Cat Fancy**, Fancy Publications, Inc., Mission Viejo, CA; **A Celebration Of Cats**, Jean Burden, editor, Paul S. Eriksson, Inc., New York, NY, 1974, (Also reprinted in 1976 as Popular Library Edition paperback, Popular Library, NY. This is the first anthology to anthologize a poem by Frank Finale.)

"The Claws" first appeared in **POEM** (1976), The Huntsville Literary Association, Huntsville, AL; **COAST Magazine** (May 1984), The Valente Publishing House, Inc., Bay Head, NJ; **New Jersey Outdoors** (1995), New Jersey Department Of Environmental Protection, Trenton, NJ

"Sun Prayer" first appeared in **Z Miscellaneous** (1989), Again & Again Press, New York, NY; **COAST Magazine** (Autumn 1991), The Valente Publishing House, Inc., Bay Head, NJ

"Storm" first appeared in **Long Pond Review** (1983), Russell, Steinke, editor, Selden, NY; **COAST Magazine** (May 1984), The Valente Publishing House, Inc., Bay Head, NJ

"My Son Searching For Insects" first appeared in **Crazyquilt Quarterly** (1987), Crazyquilt Press, San Diego, CA

"Night" first appeared in **Poet Lore** (1976), The Writer's Center, Bethesda, MD; **COAST Magazine** (October 1989), The Valente Publishing House, Inc., Bay Head, NJ

"Spiders" first appeared in **New York Quarterly** (1988), New York Quarterly Foundation, New York, NY

"Crow" first appeared in **Dream International Quarterly** (1984), Les Jones, Champaign, IL

"The Geese" first appeared in **frogpond** (1995), Haiku Society Of America, Inc., New York, NY

"Gulls" first appeared in **Poet Lore** (1976/77), The Writer's Center, Bethesda, MD; **Bird Verse Portfolios** (1987), Audio-Visual Foundation, W. I. Throssell, Director, Marianna, FL); **COAST Magazine** (Autumn 1990), The Valente Publishing House, Inc., Bay Head, NJ

"Horseshoe Crabs" first appeared in **COAST Magazine** (November 1985), The Valente Publishing House, Inc., Bay Head, NJ; **Under A Gull's Wing**, edited by Frank Finale and Rich Youmans, Down The Shore Publishing, Harvey Cedars, NJ, 1996

"Unlearning" first appeared in **The Small Pond Magazine Of Literature** (1976), Napoleon St. Cyr, Stratford, CT; **COAST Magazine** (Summer 1991), The Valente Publishing House, Inc., Bay Head, NJ

"The House" first appeared in **The Small Pond Magazine Of Literature** (1978), Napoleon St. Cyr, Stratford, CT

"Sunday" first appeared in **the new renaissance** (vol. VIII; #3, 1992), Louise T. Reynolds, editor, Arlington, MA

AUTUMN:

"The Pumpkin" first appeared in **COAST Magazine** (October 1984), The Valente Publishing House, Inc., Bay Head, NJ

"All Hallow's Eve" first appeared in **COAST Magazine** (October 1985), The Valente Publishing House, Inc., Bay Head, NJ; **Negative Capability** (1986), Sue Walker, Mobile, AL

"The Tormentors" first appeared in **COAST Magazine** (October 1989), The Valente Publishing House, Inc., Bay Head, NJ

"The Age Of Faith" first appeared in **Without Halos** (XI, 1994), The Ocean County Poets Collective, Point Pleasant Beach, NJ

"Horror Story" first appeared in **COAST Magazine** (October 1984), The Valente Publishing House, Inc., Bay Head, NJ; **Phantasm** (1980), Heidelberg Graphics, Chico, CA

"In The Attic" first appeared in **Cedar Rock**, David C. Yates, New Braunfels, TX

"Mass Of Flames" first appeared in **The Georgia Review** (1969), University Of Georgia, Athens, GA, Fall 1969, (This was the first magazine to pay Frank Finale for his work—$15. for the poem.)

"Luck" first appeared in **Piedmont Literary Review** (1986), Gail White, Editor; **Piedmont Literary Review 10th Anniversary Anthology**, Donald R. Conner, John P. Dameron, and David L. Craig, editors, Piedmont Literary Society, Danville, VA, 1986

"Necromancers" first appeared in **Secrets and Mysteries: Seventh Annual Poetry Program,** Newark Public Library, 1986; **COAST Magazine** (October 1989), The Valente Publishing House, Inc., Bay Head, NJ

WINTER AND CHRISTMAS:

"Windows, Toys, & Ice" first appeared in **New Jersey Poetry Monthly** (1980), George W. Cooke, Saddle Brook, NJ; **COAST Magazine** (December 1984), The Valente Publishing House, Inc., Bay Head, NJ

"The Snowman" first appeared in **California Quarterly** (1997), California State Poetry Society, Orange, CA

"Walking On Ice" first appeared in **US 1 Worksheets** (1999), US 1 Poets Cooperative, Ringoes, NJ

"The Firs" first appeared in **COAST Magazine** (December 1984), The Valente Publishing House, Inc., Bay Head, NJ; **Maelstrom** (Winter, 1968), Student Publications Board Of Virginia Polytechnic Institute, Blacksburg, VA (This was the first magazine to feature Frank Finale's poems, eleven published in Winter 1968.)

"From The Corner" first appeared in **Dear Winter: Poems For The Solstice,** Marie Harris, editor, Northwoods Press, Thomaston, ME, 1984

"Survival" first appeared in **Poet Lore** (Spring 1974), The Writer's Center, Bethesda, MD

"Before Bed" first appeared in **ELF: Eclectic Literary Forum** (1995), ELF Associates, Inc., Tonawanda, NY

"Winter Complaint" first appeared in **The Blue Grass Literary Review** (Autumn 1979), Midway College, Midway, KY

PEOPLE:

"To My Mother" first appeared in **Negative Capability** (1987), Sue Walker, Mobile, AL

"Louie" first appeared in **The Smith** (1973), The General Association, Inc., Brooklyn, NY

"Jimmy" first appeared in **EPOS, A Quarterly Of Poetry** (1970-71), The Work of American and British Poets, Will Tullos and Evelyn Thorne, editors, Crescent City, FL, (Frank Finale's first published poem, "The Philosophers" appeared here in the Winter 1966-67 edition.); **COAST Magazine** (June 1984), The Valente Publishing House, Inc., Bay Head, NJ

"The Gathering" first appeared in **Blue Unicorn** (1991), Blue Unicorn Inc., Kensington, CA

"Plane Choice" first appeared in **Journal Of New Jersey Poets** (1990), County College Of Morris, Randolph, NJ

"Poe" first appeared in **Prophetic Voices** (1983), Ruth Wildes Schuler, editor, Heritage Trails Press, Novato, CA

"Making The Rounds" first appeared in **Awakenings, Eighth Annual Poetry Program,** Newark Public Library, 1987; **COAST Magazine** (Summer 1991), The Valente Publishing House, Inc., Bay Head, NJ

"Stranger Passing: first appeared in **the new renaissance** (vol. V, #1, 1982), Louise T. Reynolds, editor, Arlington, MA

"Losing God" appears here for the first time.

"A Love Poem?" first appeared in **COAST Magazine** (Winter 1991), The Valente Publishing House, Inc., Bay Head, NJ

"Garage Organist" first appeared in **Seascape** (1983), Ocean County College, Toms River, NJ; **Visions** (1985), Bradley R. Strahan, Fredericksburg, VA; **Anthology Of Magazine Verse And Yearbook Of American Poetry,** Alan Pater, editor, 1986-88 edition

SCHOOL:

"Last Day" first appeared in **Asbury Park Press,** 1993

"Looking For Miss Gordon" first appeared in **the new renaissance** (vol. VIII, #3, 1993), Louise T. Reynolds, editor, Arlington, MA

"Summer Recess" first appeared in **the new renaissance** (vol. X, #3, 1998), Louise T. Reynolds, editor, Arlington, MA

"Long Division" first appeared in **Hiram Poetry Review** (1976), David Fratus, editor, Hiram, OH; **COAST Magazine** (January/February 1990), The Valente Publishing House, Inc., Bay Head, NJ

"Kay Wheeler" first appeared in **The Bluegrass Literary Review** (1983), Midway College, Midway, KY

"Kenny" first appeared in **Poetry, NOW** (1980), E. V. Griffith, Eureka, CA

"Elementary" first appeared in **Footwork: The Paterson Literary Review** (Issue 24-25, 1995), Passaic County Community College, Paterson, NJ

LABOR:

"Julio" first appeared in **Phantasm** (1980), Heidelberg Graphics, Chico, CA; **Secrets and Mysteries: Seventh Annual Poetry Program,** Newark Public Library, 1986

"The Exterminator" first appeared in **The Small Pond Magazine Of Literature** (1972), Napoleon St. Cyr, Stratford, CT

"Laborer" first appeared in **New Infinity Review** (1976), Infinity Publications, South Point, OH

"Construction Worker" first appeared in **Environment: Essence & Issue** (1992), Pig Iron Press, Youngstown, OH; **Sensations Magazine** (1997), David Messineo, Secaucus, NJ

"Sign Man" appears here for the first time.

"Ritual" first appeared in **The Piedmont Literary Review** (1991), The Piedmont Literary Society, Forest, VA

Other books and periodicals where you will find poetry and prose by Frank Finale

Anthologies

Anthology Of Magazine Verse And Yearbook Of American Poetry, Alan Pater, editor, 1985, 1986-1988, and 1997 editions

Blood To Remember: American Poets On The Holocaust, Texas Tech University Press, 1991

COAST Magazine's Fifth Anniversary Collector's Edition, "The Best Of COAST", Rich Youmans and George Valente, editors, The Valente Publishing House, Inc., Bay Head, NJ, June 1989

Dan River Anthology, Richard S. Danbury, III, editor, Dan River Press, South Thomaston, ME, 1985 and 1986

Life On The Line: Selections On Words & Healing, Sue Walker and Rosaly Roffman, editors, Negative Capability Press, 1992

Movieworks, John W. Blaneied, editor, Little Theatre Press, 1990

Peace Is Our Profession, Poems And Passages Of War Protest, Jan Barry, editor, East River Anthology, Montclair, NJ, 1981

Sunlight On The Moon, Barbara de la Cuesta and Nancy Dowd, editors, Carpenter Gothic Publishers, 1999

Teaching Poetry In High School, authored by Albert B. Somers, National Council Of Teachers Of English, 1999

Zoo Poems, Jennifer Welch Bosveld, editor, Pudding House Publications, Johnstown, OH, 1988

Literary and College Journals and Magazines

Audio/Visual Poetry Foundation, W. I. Throssell, Director, Marianna, FL
Bachet, Hamlet Publications LTD, Irvington, NJ
Beyond, Other World Books, Fair Lawn, NJ
Big Hammer, David Roskos, editor, Proletkult Press, New Brunswick, NJ
Bitterroot, Menke Katz, editor, Brooklyn, NY
Black Swan Review, Joe Weil, Elizabeth, NJ
Brussels Sprout, Mercer Island, WA
Circus Maximus, Pet Garrison, editor, York, PA
Colorado-North Review, Student Medic Corporation Of The University Of Northern Colorado, Greeley, CO
Cycloflame, Vernon Payne, editor, San Angelo, TX
Descant, Texas Christian University Press, Fort Worth, TX
Golden Isis, Gerina Dunwich, editor, Fort Covington, NY
Green's Magazine, David Green, editor, Regina, Saskatchewan, Canada
Jean's Journal, J&C Transcripts, Kanona, NY
Kansas Quarterly, Kansas, Quarterly, Manhattan, KS
LIPS, Lips Press, Montclair, NJ
Long Shot, Long Shot Productions, Inc., New Brunswick, NJ
New Laurel Review, Alice Moser Claudel, New Orleans, LA
Newark Public Library Annual, Newark, NJ
Owlflight, Unique Graphics, Oakland, CA
Passaic Review, Richard Quatrone, editor, Passaic, NJ
Poetry Today, Portland, OR
Road Apple Review, Road Runner Press, Oshkosh, WI
The American Poet, W. S. Tremble, editor, Charleston, IL
The Cardinal Poetry Quarterly, Eda Cascian, editor, Melrose Park, IL
The Haven, Michael McDaniel, Albuquerque, NM
The Long Story, R. P. Burnham, editor, Lawrence, MA
The Mendocino Review, Chuck Hathaway, Mendocino, CA
The Poet, The Fine Arts Society, Mishawaka, IN
United Poets, Charleston, IL
Voices International, South and West, Inc. Little Rock, AR
Wind, Charles G. Hughes, Lexington, KY
Without Halos, The Ocean County Poets Collective, Point Pleasant Beach, NJ, various editions
Xanadu, The Long Island Poetry Collective, Inc., Huntington, NY
Zahir, Diane Krunchkow, Durham, NH

Magazines

Down Memory Lane, Dobbs Publishing Group, Inc., Lakeland, FL, December/January 1993
Sunshine Magazine, Sunshine Press, Henrichs Publications, Inc., Litchfield, IL

Newspapers

The Princeton Packet

Sara Eyestone

American artist Sara Eyestone is known for her choice of beautiful subjects painted with unusual combinations of glorious colors. Art lovers and private collectors commission her paintings that later become the subject of her international art posters, calendars, lithographs, and Caspari notecards. This published work is available in over 500 museum shops and specialty stores worldwide. In 1986, when Sara's "The Golden Lady" was chosen as the official Statue of Liberty Commemorative Plate, the New Jersey State Museum celebrated her work with a large retrospective featuring paintings and drawings from her private collectors. It was the artist's fiftieth solo exhibition. Today Sara has moved her studio from the Jersey Shore to the famous Riverwalk in San Antonio, Texas. She welcomes all art lovers to visit while she is painting. A website of her work is located at www.saraeyestone.com.

Stephen Harrington

Stephen Harrington established his business, Coastal Guardians, in 1994 for the sole purpose of presenting our nation's lighthouses from an historic perspective. Each light is visited, photographed, and researched for historical accuracy. Working in cooperation with the light's historian/director, a time period reflecting the lighthouse's peak operation is selected, and the details are refined to present a rendition that is as historically accurate as possible. Each print is accompanied by a one or two page history. Stephen resides in Virginia Beach, Virginia.

Dawn Hotaling

Dawn Hotaling is a watercolor artist who captures not only the likeness of the places she paints but also their spirit. She has been commissioned to paint over 200 homes, inns, historical buildings, and other sites across the country. Her paintings have received many respected awards and have been selected for use in publications, books, and greeting cards. During the summer of 1999, Dawn will see the fulfillment of a dream in an extensive hiking trip across Iceland—an adventure full of artistic possibilities! Dawn resides in Long Branch, New Jersey. A website of her work is located at www.dawnhotaling.netmegs.com.

Paula Kolojeski

Paula Kolojeski has been painting the New Jersey Shore in pastels for over twenty years. Working on location, she enjoys capturing the effects of light on sand and sea. Her work has won awards in many juried shows and is found in collections throughout the United States as well as Canada, Europe, Saudi Arabia, and Japan. She is represented by Main Street Gallery in Manasquan, New Jersey where originals and limited edition reproductions of her work are available. Paula resides in Princeton, New Jersey.

Dick LaBonté

Dick LaBonté began to paint professionally in his fifties after he took early retirement from Business Week magazine in New York. His neo-primitive acrylic scenes of bygone days at the New Jersey Shore caught on quickly. These and other prints are sold along the eastern seaboard, from Virginia to Cape Cod. One of them, "Cocktails at the White House," depicting a gathering of all the Presidents and First Ladies, hangs in the executive mansion. He is represented by the family-owned Anchor & Palette Gallery in Bay Head, New Jersey where the artist resides as well. A website of his work is located at www.flatdisk.com/gallery.

Sheila Mickle

Sheila Mickle, an artist and art teacher, is a native of the Point Pleasant area in New Jersey. She is a graduate of Millersville University in Pennsylvania and teaches art in Point Pleasant Borough High School. Sheila specializes in pen and ink drawings and calligraphy, but also works in acrylics, watercolors, and mixed media. Her work has been displayed in local and regional juried art exhibitions, as well as many retail outlets. Her drawings and calligraphy have been featured in COAST Magazine, Notecards of the Jersey Shore, cookbooks, calendars, brochures, and in the local history book, "The People of Ocean County" by David Oxenford.

Virginia Perle

Virginia Perle has been painting and drawing since early childhood. She went on to study Fine Arts at Montclair State College in New Jersey and with renowned watercolor artists as well. She has exhibited extensively throughout the Northeast, especially in New York and Pennsylvania. Her paintings can be found in private and corporate collections, a United States congressional office, and twenty-nine foreign countries. She recently exhibited some of her work in the Rotunda of the House Of Representatives Office Building in Washington, D.C., and at the Statehouse in Trenton in a summer-long, single-artist exhibit. Her watercolors cover a wide range of subjects including landscapes, seascapes, city scenes, still lifes, and portraits. Virginia resides in Island Heights, New Jersey.

Muriel Rogers

Muriel Rogers' paintings reflect her passion for color—particularly the colors found in nature. She is widely recognized for her masterly blending and mingling of pigment to capture the fleeting effects of light and atmosphere. Her work, rendered in a combined realistic-impressionistic style, often focuses on the ever-changing colors of the sky. A native of New Jersey, Muriel spent summers with her family at the Jersey Shore and began her love of the ocean at an early age. A graduate of Georgian Court College in New Jersey, she developed her painting technique through many years of private instruction and workshops led by nationally known artists. A prolific painter, her work is collected nationally and has been featured on cable TV and in the watercolor magazine, *American Artist*. Muriel resides in Colts Neck, New Jersey.

Ludlow Thorston

Ludlow Thorston describes himself as a "truly American watercolorist," a man whose technique and individual interpretation reflect sincerity and dedication to his art. His medium is aquarelle, a transparent technique in which the white of the paper is used for light. Bold strokes, washes, and subtle dashes of color are added to produce fresh, vibrant paintings. Ludlow Thorston is a member and past president of the New Jersey Watercolor Society. A graduate of Newark School Of Fine Art in New Jersey and New York University, he is recognized as a major talent in the medium of watercolor painting. Ludlow and his wife, Nell, reside in Island Heights, New Jersey, where his gallery is located.

Margaret Tourison Berndt

Margaret travels the globe gathering reference material for paintings of unique and interesting boats indigenous to specific areas. Experiencing the moment and depicting her personal vision has become a signature element in her work and brought her acclaim as the only fine artist allowed access by the America[3] Foundation to depict the first all-women team to vie for the prestigious America's Cup. It is that same spirit which has taken her to a small island in the San Blas region of the Caribbean, where she lived in a thatched hut among the Kuna Indians studying their watercraft. A published artist, her work hangs in many corporate, municipal, and private collections. Margaret has summered at the Jersey Shore since she was a child and currently resides in Grand Haven, Michigan. A website of her work is located at www.tillerandtide.com.

Theresa Troise Heidel

Primarily painted on location, Theresa's watercolors reflect a love of architecture and keen understanding of light and atmosphere. She is a graduate of St. Peter's College in Jersey City, New Jersey and undertook postgraduate studies at the Accademia delle Belle Arti in Florence, Italy. She also studied under Ferdinand Petrie at the Ridgewood Art Institute in Ridgewood, New Jersey, where she later taught watercolor painting. Theresa's paintings have been featured in *Jersey Shore Vacation Magazine*, *The Jersey Shore Guide Book*, *Jersey Shore Home & Garden*, *Eclectic Magazine*, and on the cover of the 1995 *Monmouth County Cancer Society Ad Book Journal*, as well as in advertisements for the Monmouth County Tourism Board. Her watercolors were featured in the December, 1989 "Watercolor Page" of *American Artist* magazine. Theresa is represented by Oceanside Gallery in Belmar, New Jersey and Northridge Gallery in Ridgefield, Connecticut. She resides in Ridgefield Park, New Jersey.

Margaret Tourison Berndt   "Ellen's Dune"

36" x 48"   Acrylic   1994   Collection of North Ottawa Community Hospital   Prints Available

Sheila Mickle
"Home From The Sea"
11" x 14"   Ink   1994
Prints Available

Sheila Mickle
"Beside The Sea"
11" x 14"   Ink   1984
Prints Available